COLLEGE MAJOR QUIZZES

12 EASY TESTS TO DISCOVER WHICH PROGRAMS ARE BEST

JOHN J. LIPTAK, ED.D.

JIST Works
America's Career Publisher

College Major Quizzes: 12 Easy Tests to Discover Which Programs Are Best

© 2011 by John J. Liptak

Published by JIST Works, an imprint of JIST Publishing
875 Montreal Way
St. Paul, MN 55102
E-mail: info@jist.com

Visit our website at **www.jist.com** for information on JIST, free job search tips, tables of contents, sample pages, and ordering instructions for our many products!

Development Editor: Heather Stith
Copy Editor: Stephanie Koutek
Cover and Interior Designer: Toi Davis
Proofreaders: Chuck Hutchinson, Jeanne Clark
Indexer: Cheryl Lenser

Printed in the United States of America
20 19 18 17 16 15 14   9 8 7 6 5 4 3 2

Library of Congress Cataloging-in-Publication data is on file with the Library of Congress.

We have been careful to provide accurate information in this book, but it is possible that errors and omissions have been introduced. Please consider this in making any career plans or other important decisions. Trust your own judgment above all else and in all things.

Trademarks: All brand names and product names used in this book are trade names, service marks, trademarks, or registered trademarks of their respective owners.

ISBN 978-1-59357-867-1 (text)

ISBN 978-1-59357-880-0 (eBook)

About This Book

"What's your major?" is probably the most common question you will hear once you enroll in college. Choosing a major, however, is not an easy decision. It takes a great deal of self-reflection, information gathering, occupational exploration, and evaluation of potential alternatives. The purpose of this book is to help you walk through the stages involved in choosing an effective major for you.

From the time you step foot on a college campus, family members, roommates, friends, advisors, and professors pressure you to select a major. You may be thinking to yourself, "Do these people really want me to make a major life decision right now?!" You may be tempted to choose any major simply to relieve the pressure to make a decision.

In rushing to choose a major, however, you run the risk of making a poor choice of the best major to fit your interests, values, skills, and personality. Given the fact that once you graduate from college, you will probably work more than 100,000 hours in an occupation, it is important that you choose wisely and enter an occupation that you enjoy.

You can dramatically improve your chances of having lifelong career and life satisfaction by selecting a major that fits you and allows you to express your passions. In my work as a career counselor, I have helped many college students choose a major, and I can help you, too. I have designed the assessments in this book to help you make an informed decision about the major that will enable you to have many wonderful years working in an occupation that you love.

Acknowledgments

Writing the second book in this series (the first being *Career Quizzes*) was a challenging and rewarding experience. I thank the students at Radford University with whom I worked in formulating many of the ideas, activities, and assessments for this book. They allowed me to participate in their career development and have a tiny part in helping them make one of the most important choices of their lives—the choice of a college major. I appreciate them for letting me share in their career journey. They have taught me a great deal about the complex experience of choosing a college major and have helped me to refine my career counseling tools and techniques.

I also thank the many editors at JIST Publishing I was privileged to work with on this project, including Dave Anderson, Heather Stith, and Stephanie Koutek, for their generous contributions during the writing of this book. I appreciate their diligence in making this book read well, their attention to the details of the career counseling process, their wonderful advice and suggestions, and their devotion to making this book successful. I will be forever indebted to them for their professionalism, friendship, and editorial direction during the writing of this book. I would also like to thank Sue Pines, publisher at JIST Publishing, for her encouragement in the writing of this book. Without her support and mentoring, this book would not have been possible.

Last, but not least, I thank my wife, Kathy, for her encouragement, patience, and support during the many hours of the writing of this book. I love her very much and appreciate all she has done to help make this book possible.

Table of Contents

Introduction

Shawn knows he wants to be a pharmacist and plans to study biology and chemistry in college. Jane is less certain. She feels interested in about five different subjects but does not know which would be the most satisfying to turn into a career. Jennifer has narrowed her decision to social work or psychology, but is not sure which helping profession suits her best. John thought he knew what he wanted to study when he entered college, but has since changed his major five times and is still not totally satisfied. Sharon has no idea of what to major in and wants to put off the decision until later.

Do any of these college students sound like you? College students vary greatly in their degree of certainty about what major to choose. Choosing a college major can be intimidating, but ultimately rewarding because identifying and choosing the best major for you can lead to a lifetime of joy and career satisfaction.

I wrote this book because the choice of a major is one of the most important decisions any college student has to make. Many career professionals say that the choice of a major, and the occupations that are tied to this major, is the second most important decision a person will make in a lifetime, only second to the choice of a life partner! Because of the importance of this decision, you should engage in a logical process to make it, one that helps you assess your personal characteristics and match those to specific majors at the college you attend.

Leveraging Education in Your Career

In the quick-paced, ever-changing workplace of today, you need to find a way to leverage your education. We all have to embrace the fact that we are living in a knowledge-based society, and the people who are able to get a good education and use that education wisely (and continue to learn) are the ones who will find the most career and life satisfaction.

How Education Helps Your Career Success

You are probably wondering to yourself if learning more can actually be that powerful of an agent in enhancing your career success and earning power. The quick answer is yes! Consider these statistics provided by Georgetown University's Center on Education and the Workforce:

- The percentage of new jobs that require higher education is growing, and will continue to do so. Statistics suggest that by 2018, 63 percent of available jobs will require postsecondary education.

- People living in poverty who acquire a postsecondary education have a 41 percent lower chance of returning to government-sponsored programs than those who do not continue their education beyond high school.

- The completion of a community college degree can raise a person's income by 65 percent and increase a person's chance to become financially independent.

- The average income increases with educational attainment. According to the United States Department of Labor, over a 40-year working career, by just staying in school and graduating, workers earn an average of $8,000 per year more, or $320,000 more in their lifetimes.

- High school dropouts account for half of the households on public assistance, and more than 60 percent of the population incarcerated in state and federal prisons.

How Learning More Helps You Earn More

The following tables highlight the importance of getting as much education as possible in the workplace of tomorrow. These statistics from a 2002 report from the U.S. Department of Labor suggest that the more you learn, the more you will earn, and the more employable you will be in the workplace of the future.

Average Earnings

Following are the average earnings for American workers based on the amount of education they have attained:

Education Level	Hourly Wage	Annual Wage
Less than high school diploma	$10.47	$21,788
High school diploma	$14.87	$30,940
Some college, no degree	$16.85	$35,048
Associate degree	$18.02	$37,492
Bachelor's degree	$24.05	$50,024
Master's degree	$28.50	$59,280
Doctoral degree	$36.02	$74,932
Professional degree	$36.85	$76,648

Earning Power

The more education you attain, the more earning power you have throughout your career. Look at the startling statistics in the following table:

Education Level	Average Lifetime Earnings
Never completed high school	$1.1 million
High school diploma or GED	$1.2 million
Some college or vocational training	$1.5 million
Associate degree	$1.8 million
Bachelor's degree	$2.1 million
Master's degree	$2.5 million
Doctoral degree	$3.4 million
Professional degree	$4.4 million

The interesting fact about the relationship between education and earning power is that there continues to be a relative shortage of employees at high levels of skill, even among college graduates. Therefore, there continues to be a need for highly educated workers who are willing to embrace the notion of lifelong learning.

Downsizing Rates

The more education you have, the less likely are your chances of finding yourself being downsized and unemployed. Look at the following table:

Education Level	Unemployment Rates
Never completed high school	14.4%
High school diploma or GED	7.1%
Some college or vocational training	5.7%
Associate degree	4.0%
Bachelor's degree	3.3%
Master's degree	2.2%

Most experts suggest that these trends will continue and that the gap between college graduates and those without a degree will grow even larger as fewer and fewer jobs are available to those without any college education.

Why Commitment to Education Is Important

As the facts in the previous tables have shown, the more you learn, the more you earn! So why don't more people simply get more education and live the good life? Because getting more education is not as easy as it sounds.

If you are reading this book, you want to get the type of education that will bring you financial success and career satisfaction. To attain these, you will need to be able to identify a major that fits you like a glove. Think about some of the statements that follow:

- "How can I find out what I would like to learn about?"

- "Where should I focus my learning?"

- "How do I know which information to master?"

- "What facts and perspectives should I master?"

- "What subjects will be hot in the next decade?"

- "How should I learn something new?"

- "What would my supervisor want me to learn about?"

- "How can I learn new things if I can't afford to go back to school?"

If you are asking yourself questions like these, you are not alone. Because we live in times of unprecedented social and technological change that is profoundly affecting the nature of the work we do, we must be willing and able to learn new work-related knowledge and skills. Employees must now be able to deal with issues for which they have been trained as well as those that they may never have faced before.

According to the U.S. Department of Education, a significant number of high school students are choosing to go to college. Its research indicated that nearly 75 percent of all high school graduates enroll in college within two years of graduation. Reasons for this increase in the numbers of students attending college include fear of unemployment without a college degree, pressure from parents, and lack of significant other career goals. Not suprisingly, the research also indicates that a significant number of these students are not prepared to succeed in college.

Although students typically choose to go to college for a variety of reasons, fewer and fewer of them are truly committed to the completion of their degree. The following assessment is designed to help you explore your commitment to receiving an education and leveraging it in your career for financial security and life happiness.

The Commitment to Education Inventory

Before you choose a major, it is important that you explore your commitment to education in general. In my work with freshmen and sophomores trying to choose a major, I find that one of the reasons people find it difficult to choose a major is that they are not committed to getting a college education. Some of the reasons for a lack of commitment can be seen in the following statements by college students:

"I would rather be working."

"There is nothing offered that I am interested in at this college."

"What I want to study can't be found in college."

"I am interested in starting my own business."

"I'm just not ready to go to college yet."

"Nobody in my family has ever gone to college. How am I supposed to know what to study?"

This quiz is designed to help you identify how committed you are to obtaining and leveraging your education for success and satisfaction. Read each of the statements that follow and decide how descriptive the statement is of you. In each of the choices listed, circle the number of your response on the line to the right of each statement, using the following scale:

> 3 = A Lot Like Me
>
> 2 = A Little Like Me
>
> 1 = Not Like Me

This is not a test. Because there are no right or wrong answers, do not spend too much time thinking about your answers. Be sure to respond to every statement.

	A Lot Like Me	A Little Like Me	Not Like Me
1. I think that a college degree will greatly improve my life and career.	3	2	1
2. I learn things outside school as well as in school.	3	2	1
3. I view a college education as more than merely going to school.	3	2	1
4. College gives me tools to learn how to think.	3	2	1
5. I want to increase my appreciation for music, politics, and the arts.	3	2	1
6. I set educational goals that are specific and meaningful.	3	2	1
7. I can focus my energy on doing well in college.	3	2	1
8. I feel a lack of motivation about college.	1	2	3
9. I can visualize my ideal future in an occupation after college.	3	2	1
10. I set college-related goals that are realistic and achievable.	3	2	1
11. The life I want requires a college degree.	3	2	1
12. I believe that college will provide me with many options.	3	2	1
13. I would rather be working than going to college.	1	2	3
14. I am willing to accept short-term pain to create long-term gain.	3	2	1
15. I take action to move myself toward my goals.	3	2	1
16. I complete school assignments at the last minute.	1	2	3
17. I am self-disciplined in achieving my career-related goals.	3	2	1
18. College seems meaningless to me.	1	2	3
19. Self-exploration seems like a waste of time.	1	2	3
20. The job I want doesn't require a college degree.	1	2	3
Total: _____			

Scoring

Committing to and leveraging your education for financial success and personal and career satisfaction provide the foundation for making your choice of a major. For the items you completed on the previous page, add up the numbers you circled. Put that total on the line marked "Total" at the end of the section. To interpret that total, read the following decriptions:

- A score from 20 to 33 is low and indicates that at this point you do not feel committed to your education and to achieving the goal of completing a college degree for career success.

- A score from 34 to 46 is average and indicates that at this point you feel somewhat committed to your education and to achieving the goal of completing a college degree for career success.

- A score from 47 to 60 is high and indicates that at this point you feel committed to your education and to achieving the goal of completing a college degree for career success.

The one thing I have learned in my time providing career counseling services to undecided students is that the proper choice of a major will greatly enhance your motivation in college. Once you find a major that fits you, you will begin to enjoy classes, make friends with similar interests as you, and become excited about learning. If you did not score as high as you wanted on this assessment, use the rest of this book to choose a major, and you will see your educational motivation skyrocket!

The Method Used in This Book

Since the beginning of time people have been concerned about how to find greater satisfaction in life. In ancient Greece, the extraordinary philosopher Socrates had a mission to help other people seek a deeper understanding of what constituted a good life. He was dedicated to discovering wisdom within himself and drawing this wisdom out of others. His method, called the Socratic method, consisted of a series of questions he would pose to help other people explore their true nature so they could experience success.

This book adheres to Socrates' mantra that "the unexamined life is not worth living." It will help you to examine and explore the enduring qualities or characteristics you possess and how those characteristics affect your college major choice.

The Guided Self-Reflection Approach

College Major Quizzes is unlike most other books that are designed to help you choose a major, largely because it does not pretend to provide you with a magic formula for success. You have to work for it by taking the quizzes and evaluating and acting on your results.

But the quizzes in this book aren't really quizzes (not in the panic-inducing, late-night cramming sense of the word). They are self-assessments designed to help you explore your interests, preferences, values, and other personal characteristics and then apply those characteristics to your choice of a major. These quizzes can help you to recognize patterns of behavior, identify strategies that are productive and unproductive, and enrich your understanding of how you interact with the world. Quizzes provide a path to self-discovery through the exploration of your unique traits. I call this process *guided self-reflection*.

Guided self-reflection is a unique way of learning about yourself. Each chapter of this book will coach you through the following self-reflection process:

- Preparing to make a decision
- Looking at your primary attributes
- Knowing yourself better
- Developing an action plan

The quizzes in this book will help you see yourself as you really are, though be aware that they are exercises in self-exploration and not final definitions of your character or attitudes. Still, the results of this process should help you to reflect on your life, question past behaviors, find meaning, and make connections. You will be encouraged to make specific plans, set goals, and take action. After all, making a choice is the point of this book. The quizzes are simply a way of getting there.

A Word About the Quizzes in This Book

A quiz can provide you with valuable information about yourself. However, please remember that such instruments cannot measure everything about you. The purpose of these quizzes is not to pigeonhole you, but to allow you to explore your personal preferences and characteristics and how they impact your career development. Remember, too, that this book contains *quizzes* and not *tests*, at least not in the traditional sense. Traditional tests measure knowledge or whether something is right or wrong. For the exercises in this book, there are no right or wrong answers. These quizzes ask only for your opinions or attitudes about critical issues in the choice of a college major.

Also keep in mind that the quizzes in the book are based on self-reported data. In other words, the accuracy and usefulness of the information is dependent on the information that you provide about yourself. You may not learn much from taking some of these assessments, or you might verify information that you already know. On the other hand, you may uncover information that might be keeping you from being as happy or as successful as you might be.

All of the quizzes in this book are designed to be administered, scored, and interpreted by you. They are merely a starting point for you to begin learning more about yourself and how you fit into the world. You may not always agree with the outcomes of all quizzes. Do not get upset. Remember that this is merely an exploratory exercise and not a final definition of who you are or what you believe. Lastly, the quizzes are not a substitute for professional assistance. If you feel you need additional help, please consult a professional career counselor in your school's career services office.

As you complete the quizzes in this book, remember to do the following:

- Take your time completing them. There is no time limit, so work at your own pace. Allow yourself time to reflect on your results and how they compare to what you already know about yourself.

- Honestly complete the exercises that are included after each quiz. These exercises will allow you to explore how the results of each quiz can be integrated into your personal and career development.

- Find a quiet place where you can complete the quizzes without being disturbed.

- Quizzes are powerful tools—so long as you are honest with yourself. Take your time and be truthful in your responses so that your results are an honest reflection of *you*. Your level of commitment in completing the quizzes will determine the levels of success that you achieve.

- Before completing each quiz, be sure to read the instructions. All of the quizzes have similar formats, but they have different scales, responses, scoring instructions, and methods for interpretation.

- Finally remember that learning about yourself should be *fun*. Don't stress over the quizzes or the results. Just learn as much about yourself as you can. You will enjoy taking the quizzes, and you will learn a lot about yourself.

Many people spend a lifetime and are never able to find career success and achieve their dreams. We all have our own definition of success, whether it's having a lucrative career, becoming renowned for our work, owning our own business, or helping other people. This book will help you choose a college major, and then find ways to implement that major for financial success and job satisfaction. Choosing a major is not difficult, but it does require some work on your part. This book is designed to walk you through a tried-and-true process for choosing a major. Be faithful to the process and you will be rewarded by finding a major that is specifically designed to enhance your career and life satisfaction.

PART 1: PREPARE TO MAKE A CHOICE

"You are now at a crossroads. This is your opportunity to make the most important decision you will ever make. Forget the past... Who are you now? Who have you decided to become? Make this decision consciously. Make it carefully. Make it powerfully."

—Tony Robbins

CHAPTER 1

Deal with the Pressure of Choosing

In an economy in which there is increasingly more competition for fewer available jobs, college graduates are often finding themselves unemployed or underemployed after graduation. At one time, it did not really matter what type of degree that college graduates received. There were plenty of jobs for them, regardless of college major. As corporations and the government have begun to downsize employees, however, it has become increasingly more important that college students choose a major that suits them and then find ways to leverage that major to become employable upon graduation.

In addition to the external pressure to choose a college major due to a failing economy, a lack of available jobs, and an increase in qualified job candidates, college students often feel pressured into making the choice of a major by their academic advisors, professors, career center staff, family, friends, or many other sources. Although all of these constituencies are truly concerned that students get into a major as quickly as possible, sometimes this type of pressure can work against students in this process. After a while, students' fears and anxieties can become motivators to make choices about a major. As a motivator, however, pressure tends to drive people to make choices before they are ready to do so.

Pressure and stress affect everyone—particularly college students like you who are attempting to choose a major. Part of this pressure, and the stress associated with it, comes from you while some of it comes from people with whom you interact while you are in college. With every passing day, the pressure is mounting for you to make a decision and begin working toward your chosen degree. The problem is that this decision is not a small one, but rather one that will influence how you live the rest of your life. This chapter offers a quiz to help you assess the level of stress you are experiencing as a result of being undecided about your major. The rest of the chapter then provides proven techniques to help you manage that stress.

The Anxiety of Being Undecided

Sally came to me in her freshman year with thoughts of dropping out of college. She said, "I need to find a major, any major!" When I asked her why the rush, she said that she just needed people to get off her back. She told me that she was having trouble sleeping and was not enjoying her classes. After I asked her more about her situation, Sally exclaimed that the pressure to choose a major was "stressing me out!" We talked about where the pressure to choose a major was coming from and how she could better handle the stress.

Sally talked about not having any interests and not being good at anything. She was in a perpetual cycle of not being able to make a decision about a major because she did not have enough information about her skills and interests, so she continued to experience increased anxiety, which in turn made the decision even harder. Like Sally, many freshmen and sophomores in college continue to feel the stress of making a choice about a major until they do so just to make a decision and relieve some of the stress. However, the problem with this approach is that, if you happen not to choose a major that fits you personally, your level of stress will increase again when you do not like the classes being taught in that major.

CHARACTERISTICS OF UNDECIDED STUDENTS

Some of the characteristics of students who are unable to make a decision about a college major include

- High levels of anxiety
- Inability to commit to decisions
- Identity confusion
- Low self-esteem
- Poor decision-making skills
- Career immaturity
- Lack of autonomy

According to the research, high levels of anxiety can be both the cause and effect of the other characteristics. Thus, college students in the process of choosing a major need to do as much as they can to reduce the levels of stress in their lives.

All people experience anxiety in their lives depending on the situation in which they find themselves. As a college student, you are under a considerable amount of pressure to choose the right major. That is understandable in light of the fact that you probably will be working in excess of 100,000 hours in your lifetime. Given that much time and commitment on your part, it is essential that you find the major that supports a job that you will enjoy doing for that amount of time.

Anxiety seems to be one of the biggest roadblocks to students trying to make the decision about a major. This phenomenon, known as choice anxiety, can be a never-ending cycle in which stress continually mounts (see Figure 1.1).

As you can see in Figure 1.1, choice anxiety occurs in a cycle until you make the choice of a major. The major components of this cycle occur when

> **N O T E**
>
> In his book *No More Dreaded Mondays* (Crown Publishing, 2008), Dan Miller says that given the amount of time that we spend working, failure to find a job in which you can express your talents, hopes, and dreams will reduce your work to merely something to pay the bills. Miller goes on to say that failure to find meaningful, significant work is not just a minor setback, it is a deeper kind of failure. This failure is one that can affect you personally, physically, psychologically, and spiritually.

1. You have a big decision to make and the decision becomes overwhelming.

2. Your inability to reach a decision provokes feelings of anxiety in you.

3. You get societal and environmental pressure to make a choice, which then just intensifies the anxiety you feel.

4. Your anxiety quickly turns to stress that affects other aspects of your life, such as your ability to concentrate in class, sleep at night, eat properly, and experience effective interpersonal relationships.

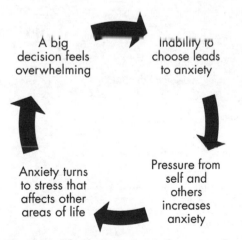

Figure 1.1: The choice anxiety cycle.

According to the research, the more undecided you are about choosing a major, the greater your level of stress is. Research also backs up the point that a heightened state of anxiety greatly inhibits your ability to choose a major.

Given all this gloom and doom, it is no wonder that you are feeling a bit anxious and stressed about choosing a major. The good news is that anxiety is a temporary condition that you can cope with and that will lessen as you get closer to making your decision about which major to study. Until then, coping strategies, which are an important mediator on anxiety and stress in the career decision-making process, are included in this chapter to help you relax until you make your final choice of a major.

The College Major Stress Assessment Scale

Before we get too far, let's see exactly how stressed you are about making the most important decision of your college career—the choice of a major. The following quiz is made up of 20 items describing the stress you are experiencing in making the selection of a good major for you. Respond to each item using the following scale:

> 3 = Very True
>
> 2 = Somewhat True
>
> 1 = Not True

Keep in mind that this is not a test. There are no right or wrong answers. Be sure to respond to every statement.

	Very True	Somewhat True	Not True
1. I am tired of thinking about deciding on a major.	3	2	(1)
2. I think about the college major decision all the time.	3	(2)	1
3. I am having trouble sleeping.	3	2	(1)
4. I am having trouble eating.	3	2	(1)
5. I am nervous all the time.	3	2	(1)
6. I don't have anyone to talk with about the college major decision.	3	2	(1)
7. I use stimulants to help me avoid thinking about my major.	3	2	(1)
8. I feel confused a lot of the time.	3	2	(1)
9. I keep going over options in my mind.	3	2	(1)
10. I am having trouble concentrating in class.	3	2	(1)
11. I can't think of anything else.	3	2	(1)
12. I don't trust my instincts about my decision.	3	2	(1)

	Very True	Somewhat True	Not True
13. I am not good at making decisions.	3	(2)	1
14. The decision is affecting my health.	3	2	(1)
15. I am getting ill a lot.	3	2	(1)
16. I get angry when I can't decide on a major.	3	2	(1)
17. I get depressed because I can't decide on a major.	3	2	(1)
18. I feel stressed a lot of the time.	3	2	1
19. I feel like a failure because everyone else has decided.	3	2	1
20. I get frustrated a lot.	3	2	1
Total: _____			

Now add the scores you circled and put that total on the line marked "Total" at the end of the assessment.

Scoring

Scores from 20 to 33 indicate a low degree of stress related to choosing a major. If you scored in the low range, then you seem to be successfully managing your stress while you work at choosing a major. You may want to skim or skip the rest of this chapter and go directly to Chapter 2 for more ideas to help you in making your choice about the best major for you in college.

Scores from 34 to 46 indicate that you are experiencing an average degree of stress related to choosing a major. If you scored in the average range, then you should continue to manage your stress while you work at choosing a major. Read the rest of this chapter for ideas about new ways to manage your stress. Then read the rest of the book for help in making your choice about the best major for you in college.

Scores from 47 to 60 indicate a high degree of stress related to choosing a major. If you scored in the high range, then you should take some measures to manage your stress while you work at choosing a major. The rest of this chapter provides proven techniques that will help you manage your stress better. The rest of the book will definitely help you in making your choice about the best major for you in college.

Stress Management

Do you find yourself wanting to choose a major just so people will quit asking if you have chosen a major yet? The following sections describe some stress management techniques you can use to reduce the stress and anxiety associated with making the choice of a major in college. Of course, stress management is not a one-time skill that you will use only during this period of time when you are trying to choose a major. It is a skill that you will use again and again.

Staying in the Present

Much of the stress that you are experiencing comes from dwelling on the past or worrying about future events. To reduce and ultimately stop these thoughts, you need to start living in the present moment. When you do this, all of your attention becomes focused on what you are currently doing.

While you are reading this book and going through the decision-making process, focus on your current classes and responsibilities in college. As you begin to focus your attention, you will notice that thoughts of the past and future will arise. When these thoughts do enter your conscious awareness, note them and gently turn your awareness back to the present. Try it for a few days and see whether it helps to lessen your anxiety about choosing a major.

Using Affirmations

All people have an internal dialog taking place in their minds. This internal dialog, referred to as self-talk, can keep you constantly thinking about your inability at this point to choose a major. For you, this self-talk probably consists of negative, critical statements related to your current situation. This self-talk tends to increase your feelings of anxiety and stress. Some of the best tools to use to combat this negative self-talk are positive affirmations.

Positive affirmations are phrases you can use to reprogram your negative, critical mind by sending it a message that the desired result has already been achieved. The following are examples of affirmations you might use:

> "I am able to manage my stress effectively."
>
> "My stress is disappearing."
>
> "I will not let stress take over my life."
>
> "I have control over the stress in my life."
>
> "I am in the process of making my decision."
>
> "I am choosing a great major."

Visualizing

Visualization, also called mental or guided imagery, is used to reduce mental activity, manage stress, induce deep relaxation, and relieve tension. The following exercise is a typical visualization you may want to try when you feel stressed about choosing a major.

PRACTICING VISUALIZATION

Close your eyes and imagine yourself walking with someone through the forest. You can hear the wind swishing through the trees as you walk and feel the wind gently touching your face. You can hear birds singing and see the deep blue sky above the trees. As you continue walking, you see a beautiful lake. You walk toward the lake and find yourself in the middle of a small patch of grass. It is quiet here; the water is perfectly calm. You take off your shoes and socks, and the grass feels soft beneath your feet. You lie down on the grass and close your eyes, feeling the sun on your face. You are completely relaxed, at peace with yourself and the world. You feel yourself drifting off to sleep. Allow your mind to take in the smells and sounds of this relaxing place.

How do you feel after completing this visualization?

_____

_____

_____

Although this visualization works for me, it does not work for everyone. Some people find relaxation at the beach or the mountains or maybe even an amusement park. Write about what type of place you go to when you need to relax:

_____

_____

_____

_____

Use this description to create your own visualization exercise.

Breathing

Because breath is vital to life itself, proper breathing is important; it also can be an excellent form of stress reduction. When you encounter stressful situations, your breathing quickens and becomes more shallow. Slowing the pace at which you breathe and increasing the depth of your breathing, therefore, can relax you and reduce stress. Diaphragmatic breathing, in which you take in long, deep breaths, is an especially powerful tool for relaxation. In diaphragmatic breathing, you push out your stomach and draw in a long, deep breath. Then you exhale as slowly and as long as possible. Repeat this cycle until you feel relaxed.

Exercising

Exercise is another excellent method for combating and managing stress. Putting aside time each week in order to exercise your body and relieve tension is important, although it can be a challenge to find this time.

Several different types of exercises are available for you to use in reducing stress:

- Aerobic exercise uses sustained, rhythmic activity primarily involving the large muscles in your legs. Aerobic exercises include such activities as jogging, running, brisk walking, swimming, bicycling, kickboxing or other high-intensity martial arts, and aerobic training. The goal of aerobic exercise is to gradually increase your stamina and enhance your cardiovascular system.

- Low-intensity exercise is used to increase muscle strength, enhance flexibility, and quiet your mind. Low-intensity exercises include slow walking, light gardening, yoga, walking in the woods, calisthenics, and "soft" martial arts such as tai chi.

For both types of exercise, especially the aerobic exercise, you should start out slowly and increase the amount of time you spend. Wellness experts recommend approaching exercise gradually. You should set limits at the beginning, such as exerting yourself for only 10 minutes every other day for the first week and then adding 5 minutes to your workout time each successive week until you reach 30 minutes per session. Make a commitment to stay with your exercise program throughout the process of choosing a major.

PLANNING FOR EXERCISE

Answer the following questions to begin your exercise program:

What types of aerobic exercise would you like to do?

_____

What types of low-intensity exercise would you like to do?

_____

When can you exercise each week?

_____

Total Body Relaxation

Anxiety manifests itself through physical symptoms in your body. These physical symptoms often reinforce your anxiety-producing thoughts and feelings. *Total body relaxation* (often called *progressive muscle relaxation)* is a simple technique used to stop anxiety by relaxing all of the muscles throughout your body one group at a time.

Progressive relaxation helps you to bring relaxation to all parts of your body through concentrated awareness. It allows you to produce relaxation by focusing self-suggestions of warmth and relaxation in specific muscle groups throughout the body.

TRYING TOTAL BODY RELAXATION

In this exercise, start with your feet and progressively relax all the parts of your body. This will help you to manage your stress effectively. Read through the following script several times before you attempt to do total body relaxation. You could also record the script and play it back as you practice this technique.

Take a few deep breaths, and begin to relax. Get comfortable and put aside all of your worries. Let each part of your body begin to relax, starting with your feet. Imagine your feet relaxing as all of your tension begins to fade away. Imagine the relaxation moving up into your calves and thighs. Feel them beginning to relax. Allow the relaxation to move into your waist. Your entire body from the waist down is now completely relaxed. Continue now to let the relaxation move into your hips and stomach. Let go of any strain and discomfort you might feel. Allow the relaxation to move into your chest until your chest feels completely relaxed. Just enjoy the feeling of complete relaxation. Continue to let the relaxation move through the muscles of your shoulders, then spread down into your upper arms, into your elbows, and finally all the way down to your wrists and hands. Put aside all of your worries. Let yourself be totally present in the moment and let yourself relax more and more. Let all the muscles in your neck unwind and let the relaxation move into your chin and jaws. Feel the tension around your eyes flow away as the relaxation moves throughout your face and head. Feel your forehead relax and your entire head beginning to feel lighter. Let yourself drift deeper and deeper into relaxation and peace.

Find a quiet location where you can practice total body relaxation. Sit in a comfortable position. Take off your jewelry and glasses so that you are totally free. Close your eyes and start to feel your body relaxing. Block any distractions out of your mind as you concentrate on relaxing your entire body. Think of yourself as a rag doll. Let the relaxation pass through each organ and body part you have. Try just to let the relaxation happen without having to force it. If during the relaxation you lose concentration, don't worry about it. Just begin again. Do this until you are totally relaxed from your head to your feet.

Meditating

Meditation is the practice of attempting to focus your attention on one thing at a time. You use repeated mental focus to quiet your mind, which in turn quiets your body. In meditation, focusing on one thing allows your mind to stay concentrated and excludes all other thoughts. There are many different forms of meditation. You can focus by repeating a word such as *ohm;* count your breaths by saying "one, two, three" when you exhale; or gaze at an object such as a candle or a piece of wood without thinking about it in words.

Cognitive Restructuring

Cognitive restructuring is the process of changing the way you view your current situation by changing your negative thoughts to positive thoughts. Such thought patterns are often referred to as self-talk. *Self-talk* includes the thoughts that pop into your head as if you were conversing with yourself. All people have these thoughts.

Negative self-talk often takes one of three forms:

- *Worriers* are obsessed with saying, "What if…?": What if I don't choose the right major? What if my parents don't like my choice of a major?

- *Perfectionists* are obsessed with saying "I should…" and "I must…": I should have chosen a major by now. I must decide on a major quickly.

- *Critics* are obsessed with saying "I can't…": I can't make good decisions. I can't understand the process of choosing a major.

TRANSFORMING NEGATIVE SELF-TALK INTO POSITIVE SELF-TALK

You can turn negative self-talk into positive self-talk. Think about the type of negative self-talk that tends to be present in your life. Then list some of the positive thoughts you can change these negative thoughts to.

List some things you say to yourself when you are worrying:

What if _____

What if _____

Now turn these worries into positives. For example, "What if I don't choose the right major?" can be changed to "I'll make the best decision given the information I have about myself and the world of work."

Write your positive thoughts here:

_____

_____

_____

List some perfectionistic things you say to yourself:

I should _____

I must _____

Now turn these perfectionisms into positives. For example, you can change "I must decide on a major quickly" to "I'm going to take my time and make the best possible decision."

Write your positive thoughts here:

_____

_____

_____

List some critical things you say to yourself:

I can't _____

I can't _____

Now turn these criticisms into positives. For example, "I can't make good decisions" can be changed to "I make decisions as well as other people my age!"

Write your positive thoughts here:

_____

_____

_____

Improving Nutrition

Many people admit that during high-stress periods they eat more than usual and eat less-healthy foods. A poor diet contributes negatively to your reactions to stress and stressful situations. Although there is no best diet for every person, following are some general guidelines to help you eat healthier at all times:

- Reduce the fat in your diet.

- Eat a balanced diet with sufficient calories, vitamins, and minerals.

- Do not eat excessive amounts.

- Reduce cholesterol consumption.

- Increase consumption of protein sources, such as fish, poultry, nuts, lean meats, and low-fat dairy products.

- Eat foods low in sodium.

- Eat fewer foods with high amounts of refined sugar.

- Avoid excessive alcohol consumption.

- Eat plenty of fruits and vegetables.

- Be aware of how stress affects your personal eating habits.

Listening to Music

Listening to music is probably one of the easiest forms of relaxation. To benefit the most from this technique, select music that is soothing and that you find peaceful and listen to it for an uninterrupted one-half hour by yourself daily.

Exploring Who Is Pressuring You and Why

You can reduce your stress by identifying the source of the pressure to choose a major. Exploring who is pressuring you to make the choice of a major and why the pressure is being applied is important.

IDENTIFYING SOURCES OF STRESS

In the table that follows, identify who is pressuring you in the left-hand column, and in the right-hand column identify why they are pressuring you. You may include yourself in this table if you are putting undue pressure on yourself to choose a major.

Who Is Pressuring You	Why They Are Pressuring You

What trends do you see?

_____

_____

_____

Choosing a college major is one of the most stressful choices you will ever have to make. The pressure to make a decision in a reasonable time frame can cause you to experience high levels of stress. This stress, in turn, makes it more difficult to make a decision. Thus, you get caught up in a choice anxiety cycle that perpetuates your indecision. The stress management techniques you learned to use in this chapter will help you while you are reading this book and working through the decision-making process. Remember that when you have reduced the stress in your life, you clear the way to make a great decision about which major to study at your college or university.

CHAPTER 2

Overcome Barriers to Choosing

When you think about the task of choosing a major in college, you can become overwhelmed. After all, everyone is probably telling you how this is one of the most important decisions you will ever make and how critical it is for you to make a great choice. When you hear things like this, it can stop you from engaging in the choice of a major. Even though it is an important decision, you should not let its importance become a barrier to your choosing of a college major.

I worked with one student, Jerry, who said that he wanted to take a course in about 10 different majors before he made a choice. Although testing out college major ideas by taking courses in areas of interest is important, Jerry would probably not be able to graduate in four years if he only used this strategy, based on the number of interests he had. I convinced Jerry to complete some of the assessments in later chapters of the book, talk to other students, and do some Internet research to complement his strategy of exploring various majors by taking coursework in them.

Similarly, I work with many students who are so afraid of making a "bad" decision that they do not make a choice at all, and some that simply keep putting the decision-making process off until the last minute. All of these reasons for not choosing a major are considered barriers in choosing the major that best fits your personal characteristics. The quiz in this chapter is designed to help you explore those barriers that might be keeping you from choosing the major that you will be externally and internally motivated to complete. The rest of the chapter provides explanations and exercises to help you overcome these barriers.

Decision Time

You have made many decisions to get where you are now. Some of these decisions have probably worked out well, and others maybe didn't work out at all. The truth is that you are constantly being asked to make decisions, and each of these decisions affects where you are now and where you will go in the future.

Decisions such as which courses to take in high school, whether to get involved in community activities, whether to go to college or straight into the workforce, what type of training to get, and even whether to work overtime can all have an impact on your career. Though there is no denying the impact of past decisions to shape who you are and where you stand in your career, most likely you are more concerned with the decision you need to make now. As you are reading this book, you are probably in the midst of trying to choose a major or soon will be. The following sections describe the basics of decision making to start you on your way to choosing a college major.

Making Career Decisions

Our careers are a constellation of decisions and their consequences. Should I take a class in psychology? What should my college major be? Do I want to be a teacher or a social worker? Should I start my own business? Should I plan to get a master's degree? These are just some of the types of career decisions that people make during their freshman and sophomore years in college. Such career decisions are difficult to make for several reasons:

- **Most career decisions involve risk.** Your entire life and your career path will change based on your career decisions. The decision you are about to make involves a certain amount of risk. For example, the wrong decision about a major may force you to stay in college longer than you expected while you change majors. Although these consequences aren't assured, they are likely, and they are risks that need to be considered.

- **Most career decisions are uncertain.** If you always knew that doing A would lead to B, then career decisions would not be difficult. However, A has a nagging tendency to jaunt off to C, D, or E instead. If you decide to major in business while in college, you are assuming that there will still be a plethora of jobs available in the corporate sector. This assumption is true most of the time. However, there are business majors who are still trying to find a job or who are underemployed in the current economy.

- **Outside influences affect career decisions.** Sometimes you can make career decisions based on what is best for you. At other times, your life may get in the way of your career decision making. For example, relationship issues or family issues can distract you from making an effective decision about a major.

The key to making successful career decisions, and in particular the decision about your major, is to reduce the uncertainty, risk, and fear that comes with them. The best way to do that is to use a rational decision-making strategy, such as the one outlined in this book.

OTHER PEOPLE'S EXPECTATIONS

When making a decision about a college major and career, some people are worried that others will say such things as

- "Only men go into that occupation."

- "Only women go into that occupation."

- "You can't make any money with a _____ degree."

- "Dumb people go into that major."

- "There are no jobs for someone with a _____ degree."

Remember that this is your life and you need to make a decision that works for you. Don't let the remarks of other people influence you too much. It's okay to listen to the advice and suggestions of others, but do not let your thoughts about what significant others might think affect your ultimate decision. Often times, we let our imaginations run wild worrying about what others will think about our decisions that we don't do what's in our best interest.

For example, one undecided student I worked with, Jimmy, told me that his father and brother were attorneys. Jimmy, however, had an interest in recreational therapy; he wanted to help people with disabilities through sports and recreational activities. He knew this was the best major for him, but he told me that he could never go home and tell his mother and father that he wanted to major in recreational therapy. He said, "They would laugh at me and probably disown me!"

I suggested to Jimmy that he really didn't know what they would think. I reminded him that it was his life and he needed to do what made him happy. I told him that once they knew about his interests in helping children, they might surprise him with their support. And surprise him they did. They told him that they wanted him to be happy, whether it was working as an attorney or a recreational therapist.

Getting Ready to Decide

Many career development experts agree that good decision making can take place only when you are ready to make a decision. Though that sounds like common sense, you might be surprised by how often people make career decisions without preparing themselves mentally for the process. Making a decision about your major without first having the proper mindset is like going white-water rafting without paddles. You could use your hands or hope the current carries you along, but it will be much harder to navigate.

In achieving a state of readiness to make career decisions, you must

- Overcome a desire to procrastinate.

- Overcome a fear of taking risks.

- Overcome a fear of failure.

- Overcome a desire for perfection.

Such fears and desires can act as attitudinal blocks, barriers to the decision-making process. The more of these attitudinal blocks you possess, the less likely you are to be ready to choose a major. Such mental barriers are caused by beliefs or ideas that you have developed over time since childhood and that continue to affect your thinking today. Psychologist Albert Ellis suggested that such beliefs are based on our notions of success and failure and can greatly affect our decision-making ability. He cautioned that it is not what happens to us in life that triggers our emotions; rather it is what we *think* about what happens that causes us to feel certain ways.

Take a look at Figure 2.1. Suppose that your professor says that you need assistance with your writing skills (A). When you experience feelings of anger and depression (C), you believe it is because of the feedback you just received. In reality, Ellis suggested, it is not the event itself that causes you to feel angry and depressed, but it is what you think about the event (B) that triggers the feelings. In other words, it's not the feedback—it's how you take it. In this example, you may begin to think such things as "I'm not cut out for college" or "I will never graduate" when in reality the professor may have just been trying to give you constructive criticism.

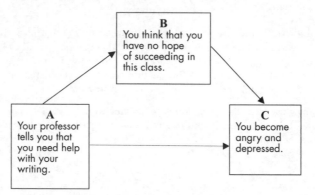

Figure 2.1: Thoughts about a comment triggering negative feelings.

Ellis suggested that we are able to control our feelings by monitoring the thought patterns that occur during certain events. Imagine the same situation with a different type of thinking (see Figure 2.2). You are told by your professor that you need assistance with your writing skills (A). This time, however, you see this feedback as an opportunity to improve yourself and something you can work on with assistance from the staff of the learning center on campus (B). You feel relieved and excited about the opportunity for improvement that the comment presents, and you appreciate the professor's attempt to help you become a better student (C).

According to Ellis, the secret in controlling your emotions is to begin becoming aware of and altering the thoughts that immediately follow any event. The key is to be aware of your emotions and thought patterns and to shift your way of thinking so that you are empowered to take action and make the best decision possible.

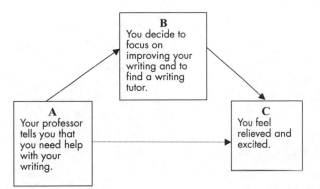

Figure 2.2: Thoughts about a comment triggering positive feelings.

Barriers to Choosing a Major Scale

This assessment contains 40 statements that are potential barriers to choosing a major. Read each of the statements and decide whether the statement describes you. If the statement *does* describe you, circle the number in the True column. If the statement *does not* describe you, circle the number in the False column.

This is not a test—there are no right or wrong answers. Do not spend too much time thinking about your answers. Your initial response will be the most true for you. Be sure to respond to every statement.

	True	False
In making a decision about choosing a major,		
1. I wait for circumstances to decide for me.	2	1
2. I have tried not to postpone the decision.	1	2
3. I leave it to others to decide for me.	2	1
4. I put it off out of fear.	2	1
5. I know who I am and what I want in my career.	1	2
6. I try to account for every possible outcome.	1	2
7. I have too many interests and abilities to decide.	2	1
8. I find fault with all possible alternatives.	2	1
9. I feel motivated and energized.	1	2
10. I make excuses for why the time is not right.	2	1
Section 1 Total: _____		

(continued)

(continued)

	True	False
In making a decision about choosing a major,		
11. I am not very adaptable.	2	(1)
12. I avoid change.	(2)	1
13. I am not willing to make sacrifices.	2	(1)
14. I am afraid of making a mistake.	2	(1)
15. I take the easiest possible route.	2	(1)
16. I set priorities among job options.	(1)	2
17. I try to preserve the status quo.	2	(1)
18. I am not afraid of rejection.	1	(2)
19. I fear being stuck with whatever I choose.	2	(1)
20. I am anxious because this decision is a big one.	2	(1)

Section 2 Total: ____12____

	True	False
In making a decision about choosing a major,		
21. I am concerned about being judged by others.	2	(1)
22. I try not to be too hard on myself.	1	(2)
23. I have trouble living up to my own expectations.	2	(1)
24. I feel like I can never please others.	2	(1)
25. I measure success in terms of end results, not personal growth.	(2)	(1)
26. I know that my decision is not a measure of my worth.	(1)	2
27. I have an unrealistic standard to live up to.	2	(1)
28. I worry about disappointing friends and family.	(2)	1
29. I have a realistic definition of success.	1	(2)
30. I would rather not make a decision.	(2)	1

Section 3 Total: _____

	True	False
In making a decision about choosing a major,		
31. I am worried about making a perfect decision.	2	(1)
32. I am not competing with other people.	1	(2)
33. I feel like my decision will not be enough.	2	(1)
34. I must make the *right* decision.	(2)	1
35. I am afraid of making a bad decision.	(2)	1
36. I can never gather enough information.	(2)	1
37. I understand that my decision can be changed.	1	(2)
38. I get obsessed with the details of the decision.	2	(1)
39. I feel like I do not have enough time to make decisions.	(2)	1
40. I research my options ahead of time.	(1)	2

Section 4 Total: _____

Scoring

This assessment is designed to assess the barriers you face in choosing a college major on four scales: procrastination, risk, fear of failure, and perfectionism. To get your procrastination score, total the numbers you circled for statements in Section 1. You will get a score from 10 to 20. Put that number in the space marked *Total* after that section and transfer the score to the corresponding line below. Then do the same for the other three scales: Section 2 for risk, Section 3 for fear of failure, and Section 4 for perfectionism.

Procrastination (Section 1) Total: _____

Risk (Section 2) Total: _____

Fear of Failure (Section 3) Total: _____

Perfectionism (Section 4) Total: _____

For each of the scales, a high score between 17 and 20 indicates that you tend to have many barriers in that area in choosing a major. A moderate score between 14 and 16 indicates that you tend to have some barriers in that area in choosing a major. A low score between 10 and 13 indicates that you tend not to have barriers in that area in choosing a major.

Understanding the Scales

Read over the following descriptions of each of the four scales. Pay close attention to any scale you scored in the high range. Once you have a sense of the barriers that can keep you from making an effective decision, you can use the tips and exercises that follow to overcome them.

- **Procrastination Scale:** People scoring high on this scale tend to postpone important career decisions, often making excuses for why they can't get to them. They do so for a variety of reasons. They may have unclear career goals and do not know what type of job they want, they may be unclear about their personal characteristics and how they match to occupations, they may have too many interests and abilities, or they may not like any of their occupational choices.

- **Risk Scale:** People scoring high on this scale are often afraid to take the necessary risks to pursue their career goals. They are afraid of such risks for a variety of reasons, including a fear of rejection, fear of the unknown, a fear of what others might say, and the possibility that a career decision could result in an even worse situation.

- **Fear of Failure Scale:** People scoring high on this scale are afraid of not living up to their own expectations or the expectations of others. They fear that even if they do succeed that they will not be able to maintain their success. They fear that their best efforts will not be good enough. They tend to tie their performance to their worth as a human being, obsessively focus on external success, or fear that they can never live up to their full potential.

- **Perfectionism Scale:** People scoring high on this scale have unrealistic attitudes about themselves. They refuse to accept anything less than perfection in themselves and others. They would rather not choose an occupation in fear of not choosing the "right" one. They tend to obsess about the details of a decision, get frustrated in not having "perfect" occupational choices, hold themselves to rigid standards, and view career decisions as all-or-nothing propositions.

The following descriptions and exercises can help you overcome those attitudinal barriers that might keep you from choosing a major. Pay special attention to information related to any scale you scored in the high range, as those are the mental roadblocks you most need to overcome.

Procrastination: Putting Off Until Tomorrow What Needed to Be Done Yesterday

Procrastination is repeatedly putting something off because you perceive the task as being too unpleasant or unappealing. People usually procrastinate either at getting started on a task or finishing a task. Procrastination often leads to feelings of stress, guilt, frustration, or regret from not having accomplished a task.

Generally, procrastinators avoid critical career tasks largely for three reasons:

- **Anxiety:** People who experience anxiety in career decision making tend to worry over the small things. On the one hand, they often see career planning as annoying and interrupting the flow of their daily lives. On the other hand, procrastinators become overwhelmed when career decisions have the potential to have a dramatic impact on their lives.

- **Low self-esteem:** Some people have difficulty making career decisions because they have a low opinion of themselves and their abilities. As a result, they simply put off making the decision.

- **A self-defeating attitude:** People with a self-defeating attitude have a negative outlook on life. They think that no career decision they could make will ever amount to any positive change, so why even try?

When it comes to decision making, procrastinators will often put off a decision until the question goes away or someone else makes the decision for them. Procrastinators worry so much about making the "right" or "perfect" decision that they are paralyzed into making no decision at all. I often see this type of thinking when students come to me for help in choosing a major, expecting me to make the decision for them. People like this have given up on making a decision and are more interested in relying on another person, such as a friend, family member, or college advisor, to make the decision instead. That way, they do not have to take responsibility for the decision and always have someone to blame if they are not successful.

At work, some procrastinators display a higher-than-normal level of conscientiousness and the tendency to want to be perfect in all they do. Other procrastinators view their responsibilities negatively and avoid them by concentrating on other tasks. This "out of sight, out of mind" strategy works until their deadline approaches, and then they must work continuously close to the deadline in order to complete the task. On the other hand, some procrastinators are so overwhelmed by the thought of having to complete a task that they feel that they need time to relax. They convince themselves that they will eventually begin working on the task when they are fresh. This cycle continues until the deadline for task completion is approaching.

Procrastination can be a vicious cycle that can lead to unfulfilled commitments. As a result of putting things off, procrastinators often feel a sense of guilt and inadequacy. These feelings, in turn, lead to lower self-esteem or the sense that the task to be done or decision to be made is too monumental, resulting in even more procrastination.

Right now, you may be procrastinating about making the choice of a major in college. But when you procrastinate, you surrender control of your career development and put it in the hands of fate or other people. For today's high-energy, self-propelled working world, procrastination is a death sentence. By the time you get around to making the career decision, the technology will have changed, the job will be closed, or the education will be too expensive. Of course, all of us procrastinate a little bit, but when procrastination impedes your career development, it is time to face the problem. You must take responsibility for your own career!

CHECKING FOR PROCRASTINATION

If you are a procrastinator, you will find yourself holding more than one of these self-defeating beliefs. Check off the beliefs that you hold dear:

- ☑ I must be perfect.

- ☑ Everything should be easy and go like I want it.

- ☐ It is safer to do nothing than to risk failing.

- ☐ If it cannot be done right, it should not be done at all.

- ☐ I enjoy getting done right at the last moment.

- ☐ I must construct the task in my head before I complete it.

- ☐ I should have no limitations.

- ☐ There is a right way of doing things, and I will wait to do them until I figure out what that way is.

FIVE QUICK FIXES FOR PROCRASTINATORS

To overcome procrastination, try the following strategies:

1. **Rewards:** After you finish a task that you wanted to postpone until a later time, try rewarding yourself with something you enjoy.

2. **Small steps:** Break down the task you're putting off into smaller, more manageable parts that you can accomplish. Set a deadline for your smaller goal, and then move onto the next small step.

3. **Hardest part:** Take a look at what you will need to do to complete the task. Then do the hardest part first before moving to the easier parts.

4. **Punishment:** Try punishing yourself by taking away something you enjoy if you have not accomplished the task by a certain self-imposed deadline. This strategy sounds painful, but it works for some people.

5. **Several minutes at a time:** Make a plan in which you will work on the task for several minutes at a time each day. Keep a daily schedule.

EXPLORING PROCRASTINATING BEHAVIOR

Use the following worksheet to explore your own specific reasons for procrastinating and some strategies you can use to start making decisions now rather than putting them off.

What types of things do you find yourself putting off till later?

_____

_____

Why do you put these things off?

_____

_____

What motivates you to get things done?

_____

_____

_____

TAKING SMALL STEPS TOWARD A COLLEGE MAJOR

The secret to making a decision about your major is that you can break down your decision into tiny steps so that you do not get overwhelmed. Remember that, as Chinese philosopher Laozi said, "a journey of thousand miles begins with a single step." In making decisions about careers, such as choosing a college major, you can develop a hierarchy of tasks you can complete to achieve your ultimate goal. Start this process by answering the following questions:

What is the next step in your process of choosing a major?

_____

What is required for you to complete this step?

_____

Can this step be broken into even smaller steps to make it more manageable?

_____

Risk: One Constant in an Ever-Changing World

Risks are those times when your behavior exposes you to the chance of injury, loss, danger, or ridicule. Although risk taking can be threatening, it also can be exciting and provide opportunities for personal and professional growth.

Most career risks are considered self-enrichment risks because they are risks you take when you hope to enhance your career and life in some way. You may want to get ahead in your career, learn new things, gain different types of skills, or earn more money. In your case, it is taking the risk of choosing a major. Effective risk-taking skills can help you reach your goals and make your dreams come true. Such risks often open you up to failure and disappointment. However, by not taking these risks, you may feel bitter at a later point in your life. As actor Zachary Scott once said, "As you grow older, you'll find the only things you regret are the things you *didn't* do."

By nature, career risks often require personal sacrifice before you see the long-term results. That is why many people do not pursue opportunities for self-enrichment—the risk seems too high, the potential sacrifice too great. The key—as any career counselor or financial investor will tell you—is to maximize your potential while minimizing your risk. Although you must be willing to take some risks in your career, they should all be *calculated* risks. Once you know how much you are willing to risk in order to pursue career success and satisfaction, and once you have accustomed yourself to those risks, then you are ready to take them and pursue your goals.

UNCOVERING CAREER RISK-TAKING PATTERNS

Think about the career risks you have taken in the past and then answer the following questions. Doing so will help you to uncover your career risk-taking patterns:

1. What types of career risks do you tend to take most often?

   _____

   _____

2. What types of career risks *should* you take more often?

   _____

   _____

3. Are there career risks you should *not* continue to take?

   _____

   _____

4. Do the career risks you take reflect what matters most to you?

   _____

Let's take a closer look at some of the different types of career decisions you are likely to encounter:

- **Decisions with certainty:** In this type of career decision, the alternatives and their outcomes are clearly known. For example, Jake is an elementary teacher in a public school in Pittsburgh. He loves teaching and can see himself doing it for the rest of his life. He knows that if he goes back to college and takes additional coursework, he can increase his salary. Should he go back to college and take additional coursework? This is a decision with certainty. Jake is certain to make more money in the long run, but the additional education is certain to cost him time and money in the process.

- **Decisions with measured risk:** In this type of career decision, the outcomes of each alternative are not totally known, but something is known about the likelihood of success or failure. Suppose Jake begins taking some college classes in a school guidance counseling program, figuring it will help him with classroom management. As he completes his coursework, he finds that he enjoys guidance counseling. He now must decide whether to continue taking classes. He realizes that with this type of degree he might be able to find a school guidance counseling position in the future. Should he put the time, effort, and expense into completing a school guidance counseling degree even if it will not guarantee him a job working as a school guidance counselor? This is a decision with measured risk.

The likelihood that Jake can land a counseling job depends on the demand for counselors and the number of openings at the time he completes his degree. He knows he can continue teaching if he is unable to find a counseling job.

- **Decisions with uncertainty:** In this type of career decision, the outcomes are totally unknown. Let's say Jake has completed his master's degree in school guidance counseling. He has heard about some new school guidance counseling opportunities, but they are all in different states. He is interested in them, but not sure about living somewhere else. His principal has also talked to him about an opening for a vice principal in an elementary school in the next county. He thought he wanted to remain a teacher the rest of his life, but now he thinks he would enjoy a promotion. Because he knows very little about the consequences of his alternatives (he has never worked either as a guidance counselor or an administrator and both opportunities are in different schools than the one he is in now), this is a decision with uncertainty.

TAKING CALCULATED CAREER RISKS

The following exercise can help you think about your upcoming career risk of choosing a major and make it a calculated one.

What education-related risk do you want to take?

_____

_____

What fears do you have about taking this risk?

_____

_____

What resources do you need to take this risk?

_____

_____

What is your action plan for taking the risk?

_____

_____

What is your back-up plan in case the risk doesn't pay off?

_____

_____

Fears of Failure and How to Face Them

President Franklin D. Roosevelt famously said, "The only thing we have to fear is fear itself." Of course, there are also spiders, heights, poisonous snakes, elevators, public speaking engagements, failure, and unsuitable college majors. But what we should be most afraid of is letting our fears paralyze us and keep us from taking risks, making choices, and pursuing our dreams.

For example, Jenny loves her work, but when she is given "large" decisions, she gets anxious, feels inadequate for completing the project, and worries what her colleagues and supervisor are going to say about her work. Therefore, she puts off the task for as long as she possibly can, and then when she does turn in the project, she feels like she has not done her best work and should have spent more time on the project. This feeling of failure then leads to further feelings of inadequacy and low self-worth, which manifests itself the next time she is given an assignment to complete.

Fear of failure is most often experienced when the voice inside your head tells you that "you can't do it." As a result of this voice, you decide not to try whatever you were thinking of doing, and your fear subsides. Then you beat yourself up for not having tried, and you continue telling yourself that you are not worthy and not a good decision maker. Each time you do this, you reaffirm your underlying belief that something is wrong with you, and your fears continue to grow.

FACING YOUR FEAR OF FAILURE

The following questions are designed to help you reflect on your life and school experiences and identify how you block your own path to success. Answer each question with a Yes or a No:

1. Do you blow problems out of proportion? _____

2. Are you worried about what others say about you? _____

3. Do you believe that career decisions are irreversible? _____

4. Do you set unrealistic expectations for yourself? _____

5. Do you become embarrassed easily? _____

6. Do you feel that you are not as good, rich, talented, or successful as your peers? _____

Look at the questions you answered with a Yes. These are all ways that people commonly exhibit their fears of failure.

Always remember that there is no such thing as total failure when making career decisions. All aspects of career decision making build upon each other. Therefore, even if you do make and explore tentative career decisions and are not happy, you still have learned things about yourself. Much of career decision making entails trial-and-error exploration. Similarly, if you end up choosing a major that you think fits your personal characteristics and you are not happy, you still will have experienced growth as a person, gained new skills, and learned something about the kinds of things you do not want to do.

And even if your choice of a major should lead to failure of one kind or another, it is not the end of the world. It may feel like it at the time, but it really isn't. Remember that choosing a major is not a one-time decision, but rather it is a decision that you can re-evaluate at any time.

FIGHTING FAILURE WITH SUCCESS

If you have a fear of failing, you should learn to concentrate on your successes. Think about all of the success that you have had throughout your life. What have you achieved or accomplished that you are proud of? What have you done that has been recognized by others? You probably have been more successful than you give yourself credit for. Take a minute and think back on your life, and then complete the following statements:

I am or I have been successful at home when I

_____

I am or I have been successful at school when I

_____

I am or I have been successful at work when I

_____

I am or have been successful in my community when I

_____

If you seem to have trouble coming up with a list of successes yourself, ask people close to you what they think you are good at and what you have accomplished. You may be surprised by their responses.

Instead of seeing failure as evidence of unworthiness, accept it as part of the process of making career choices. All people fail at times, where they differ is how they handle their failures. Failures are viewed as the end of something. But an end often opens up the possibility for a new beginning. Failure is not only a learning experience, providing immense possibilities for personal growth, but it also is an opportunity to move on and try something new with all of the knowledge gained from the last enterprise. The next time you are faced with the prospect of something you would call failure, think of Thomas Edison—a man who held over a thousand patents for his inventions—who remarked, "I have not failed. I've just found 10,000 ways that won't work."

OVERCOMING YOUR FEAR OF FAILURE

The fear of failure is primarily related to irrational, limiting thoughts and beliefs people have about themselves, their abilities, and the decisions they need to make. When you become fearful, many times it is because of how you think about the situation. To overcome your fear of failure, you need to understand and change your limiting thinking and beliefs:

1. Examine your thought patterns to understand what is triggering your feelings of failure. By becoming aware of these thoughts, you can begin to change them.

2. When you notice that you are having negative thoughts about choosing a major, stop what you are doing and listen to the negative thoughts in your head.

3. Use the cognitive restructuring technique that you learned in Chapter 1 to change these negative thoughts to more positive thoughts. For example, if you hear yourself saying, "I need to choose a major now," you could change that thought to "making the choice of a major is important, but it does not have to be right now." Similarly, you could change a thought such as "Others have chosen a major because they are more talented than I am" to "I am as talented as my peers."

4. If trying to change your negative thoughts does not work, internally shout the word *stop* to yourself. When you do this, negative thoughts will disappear as they enter your consciousness.

Perfectionism: The Impossible Dream

Like many other things in life, a small dose of perfectionism is good, but too much causes problems. Perfectionism can motivate you to accomplish great things and drive you to persevere in the face of obstacles. The attention to detail that perfectionists show can be helpful in making career decisions. However, perfectionism in its extreme form results in the belief that anything less than perfection is unacceptable—a belief that can be harmful to your choosing of a college major. It can keep you from moving forward and completing tasks, force you to adopt an all-or-nothing mindset, and cause anxiety and low self-esteem.

Perfectionists tend to be compulsive in their attempts to reach often impossible goals. They tend to measure their entire worth in terms of how much they can accomplish and how productive they can be. This focus on performance and end results causes them to ignore the many positive results that can come from a less-than-perfect outcome.

IDENTIFYING PERFECTIONIST TENDENCIES

Reflect back on your educational and work experiences and try to identify ways that you have shown perfectionism by completing the following sentences:

I set standards that are too high, unrealistic, and unreachable when I...

_____

_____

I am never satisfied when it comes to...

_____

_____

I feel devastated about my life or career when...

_____

_____

I feel less than worthy when I...

_____

_____

When students feel that no major fits them perfectly, they use that feeling or attitude as an excuse to not choose a major at all. The truth is that nobody finds a major that is a perfect fit. People who are happiest in their majors are those who find the best possible fit and then find ways to adapt that major to fit their needs and lifestyle. The quest for absolute perfection can result only in disappointment.

To combat your perfectionist tendencies, you need to first realize that there is no "right" career decision about a major. Career decisions—and their outcomes—are simply better or worse than others. There is probably a best option available to you, but even that will have some limitations. Overcoming perfectionism requires you to revise your focus and set realistic and attainable goals. It means prioritizing those results that matter most to you and identifying those sacrifices that you are willing to make.

This doesn't mean that you shouldn't have high standards or shouldn't follow your dreams. We are all entitled to a career that is satisfying and rewarding. It simply requires you to be realistic about the kinds of careers that could be satisfying and rewarding and to realize the difficulties that could be required to get there.

TIPS FOR BATTLING PERFECTIONISM

The following tips can help you overcome perfectionism at work, at home, or in the career decision-making process itself:

- Instead of setting unrealistic and unreachable standards for yourself, establish high standards that are still realistic and reachable.

- Instead of always feeling dissatisfied, focus on giving your best effort and feeling content knowing that you have done your best.

- Instead of thinking that you will find the ideal major that is a perfect match for you, accept that you are working toward the goal of choosing a major that fits most of your characteristics.

If you have yet to make a decision about the college major that you would like to pursue while you are attending college, you may be experiencing one or more of the roadblocks that have been discussed in this chapter. Whether you are procrastinating, avoiding taking risks, having a fear of failure, or being a perfectionist about the decision, you can overcome these detrimental cognitions. Remember that Albert Ellis, the famous psychologist, suggested that these types of attitudes and beliefs con be overcome by monitoring your thought patterns. When you are choosing a major, you can facilitate the decision-making process by attempting to minimize these irrational types of thoughts. The next chapter is designed to help you begin thinking creatively about your options in choosing a major.

CHAPTER 3

Think Outside the Box

Creativity is essential in the daily life of every person. You use creativity to solve problems all of the time. You may not know you are using creative processes, but you are. For example, if you are unsuccessfully trying to balance your checkbook and come up with a solution to solve your problem, you are being creative. If you find a better way to organize your class schedule so that you can be more productive, you are being creative. Creativity also can help you in choosing a major.

Marie-Louise von Franz, a colleague of psychiatrist Carl Jung, said that unconscious discoveries occur when a complete solution to a problem or question is intuitively perceived and then checked later by logical reasoning. Answers and insights then manifest themselves through this process of organizing images and ideas. This chapter is designed to help you begin perceiving potential college majors before you begin critically thinking about them.

Left-Brain Versus Right-Brain Thinking

Most researchers encourage people to foster and encourage a combination of right-brain (creative) thinking and left-brain (critical) thinking. Both types of thinking are vital for being successful in your personal and professional lives. The power of an approach to choosing a major that uses both sides of your brain can enhance your chances of being successful.

Some of the differences between creative and critical thinking are listed in the following table.

Left-Brain (Critical Thinking)	Right-Brain (Creative Thinking)
Speech and verbal	Spatial and musical
Logical, mathematical	Holistic
Linear, detailed	Artistic, symbolic
Sequential	Simultaneous
Controlled	Emotional
Intellectual	Intuitive, creative
Dominant	Minor (quiet)
Worldly	Spiritual
Active	Receptive
Analysis	Synthesis
Reading, writing, naming	Facial recognition
Sequential ordering	Simultaneous comprehension
Perception of significant order	Perception of abstract patterns
Complex motor skills	Recognition of complex figures

NOTE

Many experts on the topic of intelligence have debated whether creativity and intelligence are part of the same process or two distinct processes. Creativity expert Ellis Paul Torrance suggested that a high degree of intelligence appears to be necessary, but not sufficient, for high levels of creativity.

This chapter focuses on using right-brain, creative thinking to tackle the issue of choosing a college major. (Later chapters incorporate methods that use left-brain thinking.) Creative thinking is using thinking skills to make new and innovative connections based on information you already have about yourself. When your mind is prepped for potential "Aha," insightful answers, you can view any new information in a different light. The purpose of the following assessment is to help you explore how creative you are.

Creative Insights Inventory

All people possess different levels of creativity. Creative people talk about thinking "outside the box" in new and innovative ways. The Creative Insights Inventory is designed to help you explore how naturally creative you are.

In this quiz, circle the number from 4 to 1 that indicates how well each statement describes you:

4 = Very Descriptive

3 = Somewhat Descriptive

2 = A Little Descriptive

1 = Not at All Descriptive

Keep in mind that this is not a test, and there are no right or wrong answers. Do not spend too much time thinking about your answers. Your initial response will be the most true for you. Be sure to respond to every statement.

	Very Descriptive	Somewhat Descriptive	A Little Descriptive	Not At All Descriptive
I am able to…				
1. Visualize and see mental pictures.	(4)	3	2	1
2. See the whole picture of something, not just its parts.	(4)	3	2	1
3. Think intuitively.	4	3	(2)	1
4. Use my imagination effectively.	4	3	(2)	1
5. See the possibilities in things and situations.	(4)	3	2	1
Section 1 Total: _16_				
I am able to…				
6. Have fun with activities and ideas.	(4)	3	2	1
7. Amuse myself in childlike ways.	(4)	3	2	1
8. Be playful with ideas.	(4)	3	2	1
9. Be spontaneous.	(4)	3	2	1
10. Go with the flow of things.	(4)	3	2	1
Section 2 Total: _20_				
I am able to…				
11. Block out the opinions of others.	(4)	3	2	1
12. Enjoy myself in the present and not worry about the past.	4	3	2	(1)
13. Work and play creatively.	4	3	(2)	1
14. Create things from scratch.	4	3	(2)	1
15. Adapt easily to changes.	4	(3)	2	1
Section 3 Total: _12_				

Scoring

The Creative Insights Inventory is designed to help you explore your potential for having creative insights by measuring you in three areas of creativity: visualization skills, playful orientation, and adaptable orientation. Add your scores within each of the three sections of this inventory. You will get a score from 5 to 20. Record each total in the space provided after each section. Then transfer your totals to the spaces on the next page.

Visualization Skills (Section 1) Total: _____ 16 _____

Playful Orientation (Section 2) Total: _____ 20 _____

Adaptable Orientation (Section 3) Total: _____ 12 _____

For each section, a low score from 5 to 9 indicates that you have not yet developed the potential for creativity in this area to help you with the choice of a major. A moderate score from 10 to 15 indicates that you have some potential for creativity in this area to help you with the choice of a major. A high score from 16 to 20 indicates that you have great potential for creativity in this area to help you with the choice of a major.

Understanding the Scales

The following descriptions for the three scales are provided to help you interpret your scores. No matter how you scored—low, moderate, or high—you will benefit from completing all of the exercises in this chapter.

- **Visualization Skills Scale:** People scoring high on this scale are able to see the big picture and all of the possibilities that exist in a situation. They are intuitive and can use their imaginations to visualize concepts and see mental pictures in their mind.

- **Playful Orientation Scale:** People scoring high on this scale have a playful, childlike approach to their life and career. They are spontaneous and able to find the flow in whatever they do. They enjoy playing with ideas and possibilities to find what works best.

- **Adaptable Orientation Scale:** People scoring high on this scale tend to live in the present, not worrying about the past and not worrying too much about what might happen in the future. They adapt easily when changes occur in their environment, and they are creative in finding new ways of adapting.

Creativity Tools for College Majors

Regardless of whether you realize it, you are a creative person. When most people think about creativity, they think about singing, dancing, drawing, writing, or playing a musical instrument. In fact, many forms of creativity have nothing to do with participation in the arts. Creative people are able to think in fresh new ways that are outside the normal realm of thinking. They are able to stretch their thinking to include less-traditional ideas in achieving their goals, such as choosing a major. Creative people are able to combine information (such as the type you learned about yourself in Chapters 1 and 2) and restructure it so that new patterns begin to emerge. They are not afraid to explore new ideas, try out new options, or create new and exciting possibilities.

As we move into assessing your interests, skills, and personality in the next section of the book, keep in mind that any ideas you generate can be helpful. For now, let your imagination take over. The more ideas you can generate, the greater success you will have in identifying a major to pursue. The following tools are designed to help you begin thinking creatively about your choice of a major.

Creative Brainstorming

One of the first things I always do with the students whom I work with is to have them begin by brainstorming potential majors of interest no matter how crazy the options sound at the time. *Creative brainstorming* is a technique many people use for generating ideas. Brainstorming is a way of producing a set of majors from which you can choose the best fit. The guidelines for brainstorming include

- **Don't judge your ideas.** When you are brainstorming ideas for a major, do not evaluate the idea yet. At this stage, no ideas are bad. Any thoughts you have might work, so simply write them down. Allow yourself to think outside the practical boundaries of ordinary thought.

- **Organize the chaos.** Now attempt to organize the ideas into categories that will be useful to you. For example, you might have groups of possibilities that could be lumped into three categories titled Working with Kids, Art, and Communicating.

- **Identify the best fit.** Look at the groups that have the most ideas.

- **Explore.** Explore ways that the other categories might be integrated into the decision-making process.

Let yourself consider wacky ideas. Sometimes the ideas that seem crazy to you at first often end up being the best alternatives. Later these choices can be verified or rejected as potential majors based on subsequent career assessments (you will take these in the next part of the book).

CONSIDERING WACKY IDEAS

Write down what you believe might be exciting majors to study. Include everything that sounds interesting to you, no matter how wacky it seems:

_____

_____

_____

_____

_____

_____

Group these ideas into several categories:

Category: _____

Related majors: _____

Category: _____

(continued)

(continued)

Related majors: _____

Category: _____

Related majors: _____

Which category has the most majors? _____

Explore the category with the most majors by searching for information in the following resources. After each resource, briefly write about what you discovered about the majors in this category:

Internet: _____

_____

College catalog: _____

_____

Academic advisors: _____

_____

Students in those majors: _____

_____

_____

Library books and bookstore textbooks: _____

_____

_____

The Journalism Method

Journalists are trained in a method of research that consists of asking a series of questions that will ensure that they have covered the entire story they are writing. You can use a similar method to help you choose a major.

ASKING MAJOR QUESTIONS

Answer the following questions to help you think creatively about the work you would like to be doing in the future:

Who will benefit from your work?

_____

_____

What will you do to benefit these people?

_____

_____

How will these people benefit from your work?

_____

_____

Where will you be using your talents?

_____

_____

Why are you doing it—what do you hope to accomplish in your career?

_____

_____

What is the major(s) that fits your answers to these questions?

_____

Sentence Completions

Sentence completions are a creative, right-brain way of thinking about various majors.

COMPLETING THE THOUGHT

Look at the sentences that follow and complete each of the questions by writing the first thing that pops into your head.

If I won the lottery, the only work I would do is

_____

I naturally do

_____

I want to be known for

_____

The work I would do even if I did not get paid is

_____

(continued)

(continued)

The only work I love to do is

_____

If I had one year left to live, the activities I would engage in include

_____

The legacy I want to leave is

_____

What is the major that is most tied to the responses you provided in this exercise?

_____

Free Association

Free association is a technique that allows you to generate words and ideas without judging them. Through full concentration, you can use associations to quiet or bypass your logical mind and allow your creative, intuitive mind to emerge.

MAKING ASSOCIATIONS

This exercise is much like the free association exercises used by psychoanalytically trained therapists. Begin by letting your mind go and allowing it to freely associate. Look at the words "College majors" below. Then, in the space provided next to the words, write a word that you associate with college majors.

College majors: _____

Continue this process until you have written 25 or more words that you associate with college majors. If you cannot think of any words, write the word "free" in the space next to the words "College majors" and continue. Keep writing your associations even if you repeat some of them.

College majors: _____   College majors: _____

College majors: _____   College majors: _____

College majors: _____   College majors: _____

College majors: _____   College majors: _____

College majors: _____   College majors: _____

College majors: _____   College majors: _____

College majors: _____   College majors: _____

College majors: _____   College majors: _____

College majors: _____   College majors: _____

College majors: _____   College majors: _____

College majors: _____   College majors: _____

College majors: _____   College majors: _____

College majors: _____   College majors: _____

What is the major that is most tied to the responses you provided in this exercise?

_____

Symbolism

Another method of quieting your logical mind is by focusing on images in your mind. Try out this method by sitting quietly in a comfortable chair. Close your eyes and begin to visualize yourself working in the future after college. Think about what you believe symbolizes what the type of work you're doing means to you. This symbol can be anything that pops into your head. For example, a teacher might visualize a classroom, and a computer programmer might visualize a laptop computer. Continue to concentrate on the image in your head for about two minutes. Afterwards, complete the following worksheet.

CONCENTRATING ON SYMBOLS

Draw a picture of the image that was in your head when you were concentrating on your work after college:

What types of occupations does the symbol represent?

_____

What college majors are associated with these occupations?

_____

Combining

Think of ways you can combine different interests in one major. For example, a person with an interest in art and writing might consider advertising. Similarly, a person with an interest in both working with kids and engaging in sports and fitness activities might consider majoring in physical education. In Figure 3.1, list two interests that you might be able to combine into one major.

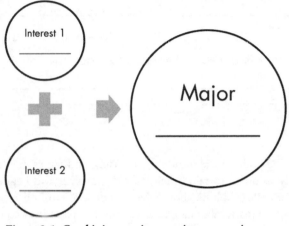

Figure 3.1: Combining two interests into one major.

You also can try combining two or more existing majors at your college or university into a third new one if your college offers an interdisciplinary major program. If you think about two majors you might enjoy, you may come up with a great major for yourself. Suppose you are interested in the music industry; you could combine coursework in music and economics into a music business major. In Figure 3.2, list two majors that you might be able to combine into one major that better fits you.

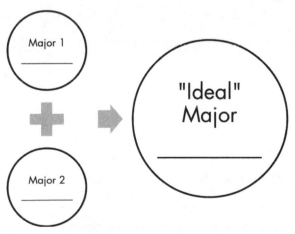

Figure 3.2: Combining two majors into a third major.

Mind Mapping

Mind mapping is a way for you to organize your thoughts about a certain topic, in this case, your college major. To make a mind map, start by writing the words "College Major" in the center of a blank sheet of paper and circling the words. Around the circle, list all of the words you can think of to describe you. Then, around each of the describer words, write other words that may be connected with the describer words. Draw lines to connect the ideas that are related. Figure 3.3 shows an example.

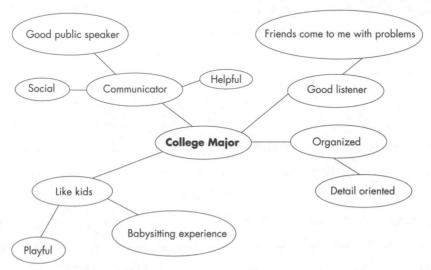

Figure 3.3: Sample mind map.

Envisioning the Future

Using imagery and picturing yourself in the future can help you to explore potentially satisfying majors and occupations.

IMAGINING YOUR FUTURE

For this exercise, imagine yourself 10 years from now, and describe what you see. How will you be living? Where will you be working? Answer the following questions about what you envision for yourself in the future:

What kind of car do you drive? _____

How many hours a week do you work? _____

Do you have to work weekends or holidays? _____

Where do you live?

_____

(continued)

(continued)

Do you own a home? What does it look like? How is it decorated?

_____

What do you do on a daily basis at work?

_____

Do you work alone or as part of a team? _____

Do you work with ideas, things, people, or data? _____

What does your personal life look like? Are you married? Do you have kids (how many)?

_____

_____

Do you work by yourself or interact with others all day? _____

Do you work in an urban, rural, or suburban area? _____

Do you live in an urban, rural, or suburban area? _____

How much money do you make a year? _____

Do you travel on your job? _____

What do you do in your spare time (hobbies, leisure activities, etc.)?

_____

Look back over your answers to these questions. What patterns do you see?

_____

_____

_____

What majors at your college or university would allow you to live this future vision?

_____

_____

_____

Congratulations! You have completed Part 1 of the choosing a major process. You have eliminated roadblocks and awakened your creative powers, and now you are ready to begin learning about yourself and applying that information to the choice of a major.

However, learning about yourself is futile unless you can critically analyze the subsequent information. People with limited critical thinking skills tend to accept or reject information without thoroughly understanding it. The good news is that critical thinking is a skill that can be taught. In the chapters in the next section, you will begin to develop the ability to think critically about yourself based on previous information and the new information you gain by completing the quizzes in this book.

PART 2: LOOK AT YOUR PRIMARY ATTRIBUTES

"The best career advice to give the young is find out what you like doing best and get someone to pay you for doing it."

—Katherine Whitehorn

CHAPTER 4

Discover Your Interests

Many people go to college for the wrong reasons and then make things worse by choosing a major unrelated to their interests. Interests are those things that hold your attention, are indicative of what you want to do, and provide proof of what you enjoy doing.

The first stage in choosing a major is to explore your interests. This chapter provides a quiz and several activities to help you do this. The thing to remember, though, is that interests alone are not enough to make an informed choice about college majors. They are just one of the three important measures that can lead to career success after college. The other two measures are your skills (which will be discussed in Chapter 5) and your personality (which will be discussed in Chapter 7).

The Importance of Assessing Your Interests

You are probably asking yourself why you need to assess your interests, likes and dislikes, and preferences for various activities. After all, you know what you like, right? Yet you're still struggling with a college major decision.

The fact is that some people don't have a good grasp on what they are interested in, and most people don't know how to translate their interests into occupations. This chapter can help you with both of these tasks. First, you can identify interests in three ways:

- **Expressed interests:** This method involves describing what you like or dislike about activities you have experienced. Although this method can be limited based on the amount of your experience, it can be a starting point for the exploration of your interests.

- **Manifested interests:** With this method, you note how much time you spend participating in various activities. This method suggests that you will spend more time in activities you enjoy and less time in those activities you do not enjoy. This method can be limited if you like certain activities, but have been unable to engage in them because of time, physical, social, or monetary limitations. However, it can again act as a starting point for the exploration of your interests.

- **Inventoried interests:** This method involves completing an assessment instrument that asks you to reflect on and record your behavior about what you liked and disliked about a variety of activities. Interest assessments are probably one of the most helpful types of career assessments available for people to take. They are the least threatening type of assessment, the most relevant for career planning, and the most easily understood and accepted by people making career choices.

EXAMINING YOUR LIKES AND DISLIKES

To start thinking about your expressed interests, complete the following table:

My Past Activities	What I Liked	What I Did Not Like

ANALYZING HOW YOU SPEND YOUR TIME

To start thinking about how much time you have spent (or are spending) in your interests, complete the following table.

My Favorite Interest Activities	Time I Spend in This Activity Per Week

_____   _____

_____   _____

_____   _____

_____   _____

Career Interest Inventory

If you already know what your interests are, why bother taking an assessment? The truth is that what you think your interests are and what the assessment will tell you about your interests are likely to be different. Interest assessments such as the Career Interest Inventory can be tremendously beneficial to your career development. Specifically they can

- Help you clarify your true interests.

- Translate those interests into college majors and occupational terms.

- Organize your interests in a meaningful way.

- Stimulate occupational exploration.

- Provide insight into the occupations you do _not_ want to pursue.

- Verify that your career goals are realistic.

- Enhance your ability to make a sound occupational decision.

- Reassure you if you already know your interests.

- Help you choose a major.

Of course, the last one is the ultimate goal of this chapter and one of the main goals of this book. Remember that the more you know about yourself, the better your odds of achieving success in your career.

The Career Interest Inventory is designed to help you explore career and job alternatives based on your interests. Read each of the items, decide how much you would enjoy engaging in that activity, and circle the appropriate response using the following scale:

    4 = Very Interested

    3 = Somewhat Interested

    2 = A Little Interested

    1 = Not Interested

NOTE

The assessment of interests began in the early 1900s when Frank Parsons, the Father of Vocational Guidance, felt the need to help young adults to begin making rational decisions about the types of work in which they were most interested. Since that time, many different types of interest inventories have been developed that are similar to the Career Interest Inventory.

This is not a test. There are no right or wrong answers, so do not spend too much time thinking about your responses. Be sure to respond to every statement. Do not worry about totaling your scores at this point.

	Very Interested	Somewhat Interested	A Little Interested	Not Interested
How interested are you in...				
1. Planting and trimming trees?	4	3	2	1
2. Managing and protecting natural resources?	4	3	2	1
3. Caring for sick animals?	4	3	2	1
4. Applying technology to farming?	4	3	2	1
5. Studying the composition of soil?	4	3	2	1
6. Conducting experiments with plants?	4	3	2	1
Section 1 Total: _____				
How interested are you in...				
7. Crafting products from wood?	4	3	2	1
8. Operating heavy equipment?	4	3	2	1
9. Working with tools?	4	3	2	1
10. Using computers to prepare detailed drawings?	4	3	2	1
11. Planning, designing, and directing construction projects?	4	3	2	1
12. Creating safe and functional buildings?	4	3	2	1
Section 2 Total: _____				
How interested are you in...				
13. Researching and writing news stories?	4	3	2	1
14. Singing in a professional choir?	4	3	2	1
15. Preparing public relations information?	4	3	2	1
16. Painting or sketching landscapes or portraits?	4	3	2	1
17. Doing commercial art or design projects?	4	3	2	1
18. Dancing in a variety show or acting in a play?	4	3	2	1
Section 3 Total: _____				
How interested are you in...				
19. Supervising and motivating others?	4	3	2	1
20. Adding columns of numbers?	4	3	2	1
21. Leading people?	4	3	2	1
22. Computing wages for payroll records?	4	3	2	1

	Very Interested	Somewhat Interested	A Little Interested	Not Interested
23. Managing a department or an organization?	4	3	2	1
24. Completing tax forms for companies or individuals?	4	3	2	1

Section 4 Total: _____

How interested are you in...

25. Teaching reading, English, or math?	4	3	2	1
26. Watching children at a day-care center?	4	3	2	1
27. Managing education programs?	4	3	2	1
28. Working with special-needs students?	4	3	2	1
29. Teaching life skills to adults?	4	3	2	1
30. Tutoring students who are having trouble in school?	4	3	2	1

Section 5 Total: _____

How interested are you in...

31. Analyzing and tracking investments?	4	3	2	1
32. Preparing financial reports?	4	3	2	1
33. Buying and selling stocks and bonds?	4	3	2	1
34. Studying financial trends?	4	3	2	1
35. Selling insurance policies?	4	3	2	1
36. Helping people plan their retirement?	4	3	2	1

Section 6 Total: _____

How interested are you in...

37. Examining financial documents for errors?	4	3	2	1
38. Making plans for land use in cities?	4	3	2	1
39. Inspecting damage from and preventing forest fires?	4	3	2	1
40. Keeping accounting records for a government agency?	4	3	2	1
41. Conducting research for crime prevention agencies?	4	3	2	1
42. Analyzing and managing information about the earth?	4	3	2	1

Section 7 Total: _____

(continued)

(continued)

	Very Interested	Somewhat Interested	A Little Interested	Not Interested
How interested are you in...				
43. Diagnosing and treating illnesses?	4	3	2	1
44. Helping people with physical and emotional needs?	4	3	2	1
45. Working as an aide in a hospital?	4	3	2	1
46. Rescuing people in emergency situations?	4	3	2	1
47. Helping people maintain healthy teeth?	4	3	2	1
48. Researching diseases and cures?	4	3	2	1

Section 8 Total: _____

	Very Interested	Somewhat Interested	A Little Interested	Not Interested
How interested are you in...				
49. Preparing and/or serving meals for others?	4	3	2	1
50. Cutting and styling hair?	4	3	2	1
51. Leading tourists on a mountain-climbing expedition?	4	3	2	1
52. Teaching tourists to scuba dive?	4	3	2	1
53. Helping people plan trips as a travel guide?	4	3	2	1
54. Managing a hotel or motel?	4	3	2	1

Section 9 Total: _____

	Very Interested	Somewhat Interested	A Little Interested	Not Interested
How interested are you in...				
55. Helping students manage stress effectively?	4	3	2	1
56. Working in a mental health clinic?	4	3	2	1
57. Helping people in crises?	4	3	2	1
58. Providing marriage counseling?	4	3	2	1
59. Doing social service work?	4	3	2	1
60. Working with juveniles on probation?	4	3	2	1

Section 10 Total: _____

	Very Interested	Somewhat Interested	A Little Interested	Not Interested
How interested are you in...				
61. Repairing computers?	4	3	2	1
62. Assisting people in using technology?	4	3	2	1
63. Managing an organization's network?	4	3	2	1
64. Writing computer programs and software?	4	3	2	1
65. Setting up or managing websites?	4	3	2	1
66. Finding new ways to prevent computer viruses?	4	3	2	1

Section 11 Total: _____

	Very Interested	Somewhat Interested	A Little Interested	Not Interested
How interested are you in...				
67. Helping people solve legal problems?	4	3	2	1
68. Using equipment to fight fires?	4	3	2	1
69. Collecting evidence to solve a criminal case?	4	3	2	1
70. Enforcing laws and regulations?	4	3	2	1
71. Preparing and arguing legal cases for trial?	4	3	2	1
72. Protecting people and property from harm?	4	3	2	1

Section 12 Total: _____

	Very Interested	Somewhat Interested	A Little Interested	Not Interested
How interested are you in...				
73. Setting up machines according to written standards?	4	3	2	1
74. Producing precision metal and wood products?	4	3	2	1
75. Operating lathes and drill presses?	4	3	2	1
76. Disassembling and repairing machinery?	4	3	2	1
77. Repairing televisions and other electronic devices?	4	3	2	1
78. Inspecting and evaluating the quality of products?	4	3	2	1

Section 13 Total: _____

	Very Interested	Somewhat Interested	A Little Interested	Not Interested
How interested are you in...				
79. Planning advertising campaigns?	4	3	2	1
80. Raising funds for an organization?	4	3	2	1
81. Persuading others to buy something?	4	3	2	1
82. Selling products over the Internet?	4	3	2	1
83. Helping people buy and sell homes?	4	3	2	1
84. Explaining and demonstrating the use of products?	4	3	2	1

Section 14 Total: _____

	Very Interested	Somewhat Interested	A Little Interested	Not Interested
How interested are you in...				
85. Solving difficult math problems?	4	3	2	1
86. Conducting chemistry experiments?	4	3	2	1
87. Collecting and analyzing rocks?	4	3	2	1
88. Studying the nature of the universe?	4	3	2	1
89. Researching and developing products for a corporation?	4	3	2	1
90. Constructing and interpreting maps, graphs, and diagrams?	4	3	2	1

Section 15 Total: _____

(continued)

(continued)

How interested are you in...	Very Interested	Somewhat Interested	A Little Interested	Not Interested
91. Maintaining automobile engines?	4	3	2	1
92. Driving a truck or taxi cab?	4	3	2	1
93. Driving a bus from city to city?	4	3	2	1
94. Doing auto body repairs?	4	3	2	1
95. Flying airplanes and helicopters?	4	3	2	1
96. Transporting passengers and cargo?	4	3	2	1

Section 16 Total: _____

Scoring

For each of the 16 sections on the previous pages, add the numbers you circled for each item. Put that total on the line at the end of each section. The higher the total number for each section, the more important it is for you to pursue those types of interests when you are making career decisions. For each of the scales, a score from 6 to 12 indicates a low level of interest, a score from 13 to 18 indicates an average level of interest, and a score from 19 to 24 indicates a high level of interest. Your results will help you focus your career direction by revealing possible majors of interest.

Matching Your Interests to Careers

Information about majors is often organized by using career clusters. The Career Interest Inventory is made up of 16 sections representing the United States Department of Education's 16 major career clusters. Those clusters, in turn, represent the majority of available college majors.

For each of the 16 areas that follow, list your score from that section of the Career Interest Inventory and whether it was low, average, or high.

1. **Agriculture and Natural Resources:** An interest in working with plants, animals, forests, or mineral resources for agriculture, horticulture, conservation, and other purposes.

   Interest: _____

2. **Architecture and Construction:** An interest in designing, assembling, and maintaining buildings and other structures.

   Interest: _____

3. **Arts and Communication:** An interest in creatively expressing feelings or ideas, in communicating news or information, or in performing.

   Interest: _____

4. **Business and Administration:** An interest in making an organization run smoothly.

   Interest: _____

5. **Education and Training:** An interest in helping people learn.

   Interest: _____

6. **Finance and Insurance:** An interest in helping businesses and people secure their financial future.

   Interest: _____

7. **Government and Public Administration:** An interest in helping a government agency serve the needs of the public.

   Interest: _____

8. **Health Science:** An interest in helping people and animals be healthy.

   Interest: _____

9. **Hospitality, Tourism, and Recreation:** An interest in catering to the wishes and needs of others so that they may enjoy a clean environment, good food and drink, comfortable accommodations, and recreation.

   Interest: _____

10. **Human Service:** An interest in improving people's social, mental, emotional, or spiritual well-being.

    Interest: _____

11. **Information Technology:** An interest in designing, developing, managing, and supporting information systems.

    Interest: _____

12. **Law and Public Safety:** An interest in upholding people's rights or in protecting people and property.

    Interest: _____

13. **Manufacturing:** An interest in processing materials into products or maintaining and repairing products by using machines or hand tools.

    Interest: _____

14. **Retail and Wholesale Sales and Service:** An interest in bringing others to a particular point of view through personal persuasion and sales techniques.

    Interest: _____

15. **Scientific Research, Engineering, and Mathematics:** An interest in discovering, collecting, and analyzing information about the natural world, life sciences, and human behavior.

    Interest: _____

16. **Transportation, Distribution, and Logistics:** An interest in operations that move people or materials.

    Interest: _____

FINDING YOUR TOP FIVE CAREER CLUSTERS OF INTEREST

Looking back over your results, which of the 16 career clusters yielded the highest total score? Use the following space to list the five career clusters you scored highest in. This list provides an excellent clue as to the kind of major you will find the most satisfaction in (and will probably be good at).

1. _____

2. _____

3. _____

4. _____

5. _____

Many people make the mistake of believing that the activities they do well qualify as their interests. Rather, you should think of interests as those activities that you are naturally drawn to or curious about. It is generally accepted that if you use your inventoried interests as a starting place in choosing a major, there is a high degree of probability that you will choose and begin engaging in a major that you will excel at. However, you need to be careful not to confuse interests and skills. The next chapter will help you explore your skills.

CHAPTER 5

Clarify Your Skills

Now that you have considered what you are drawn to and what arouses your interest, it is time to shift your focus to those things you do well—your skills. Skills are those things you have learned to do with a varying degree of proficiency. Skills can be learned and improved through application and practice.

Skills are becoming increasingly more important in the chaotic world of work. It will be critical for you to not only discover various skills that you possess, because you do have hundreds of them, but also to identify the skills you most enjoy using. Identifying your top skills can help you identify majors you will love and can excel at. This chapter's quiz will help you identify your skills and match them to potential majors and occupations.

Skills Identification

All students who are interested in choosing a major need to be keenly aware of their skills and how they can apply those skills to a variety of jobs. When I ask one of my students, Jasmine, about her skills, she talks about her seemingly natural talent for art. She has been drawing and illustrating since she was a young girl, starting with doodling and then improving this skill. She has taken some art classes in school and loved them. She describes herself as "creative and imaginative." Although making art has come naturally to her, she says that she has developed her artistic abilities over time. On the other hand, she says she is terrible at math and accounting.

In contrast, my student Paul excels at working with numbers of all types. He enjoys keeping track of the statistics for the college basketball team. He says he has always been great at math and teaching math to others. He continues to take math courses to keep getting better at it and hopes to be an actuary someday. On the other hand, he struggles with writing and often has to go to the learning center to get assistance with his assignments for English class.

Jasmine and Paul have a clear idea about their skills and what kinds of majors relate to their skill strengths. But for many, if not most, people, the connection between skills and a college major or career is not so clear. For example, I had one student come to me and say that one of the things he was best at was playing chess, but he did not know how that would help him in choosing a major. As we further discussed his skill at chess, I asked him to identify some of the reasons he is so good at chess. He provided the following answers:

- "I am able to concentrate when it is quiet."
- "I like being alone, working one-on-one against an opponent or a chess computer."
- "I am able to analyze situations during the game."
- "I think strategically, often three or four moves ahead."
- "I have memorized different ways of opening the games from both the black and white pieces and can rely on this knowledge to get an advantage."

After this analysis, he was able to see that in chess and all of the other activities he enjoyed, he was using and developing various skills. Most career experts agree that cultivating and identifying skills are important for people making the choice of a major.

DEVELOPING SKILLS IN MANY PLACES

Skills can be developed in a wide variety of settings. Think about and identify some of the skills you have learned and where you have learned them. For example, at home, you may have learned how to clean house or do yardwork. In the table that follows, list your skills and where you have gained the skills.

Where You Spend Time	What Skills You Use There
_____	_____
_____	_____
_____	_____
_____	_____
_____	_____

Most career development and job search specialists group skills into three different types:

- **Adaptive skills:** You use these skills every day. They allow you to adjust to a variety of life and career situations. They can be considered part of your personality and include such traits as patience, flexibility, maturity, assertiveness, and creativity.

- **Job-related skills:** These skills are related to a particular job or type of job. You need these skills to be successful in specific occupations. This group includes such skills as repairing a car engine, writing grants, and reading blueprints.

- **Transferable skills:** These general skills can be useful in a variety of jobs. You can transfer these skills from one occupational setting to another. They include such skills as building things, instructing people, analyzing data, leading a group, and managing money.

Keep in mind that skills can be acquired through educational experiences and leisure activities, as well as through work experiences. Transferable skills, especially, are important as they naturally develop from all aspects of life, especially from activities outside work, and then transfer to a job.

Career Skills Inventory

The Career Skills Inventory is designed to help you think about and identify the skills you possess that can be transferred to the world of work. These skills may have been acquired from working at various full or part-time jobs, leisure activities, volunteer experiences, hobbies, educational courses, and training experiences.

Please read each statement carefully. Then using the following scale, circle the number that best describes your degree of skill:

> 3 = Very Skilled
>
> 2 = Somewhat Skilled
>
> 1 = Poorly Skilled
>
> 0 = Not Skilled or Not Applicable (N/A)

This is not a test. Because there are no right or wrong answers, do not spend too much time thinking about your responses. Be sure to respond to every statement. Do not worry about totaling your scores at this point.

	Very Skilled	Somewhat Skilled	Poorly Skilled	Not skilled or N/A
In handling plants and animals, how skilled are you at the following tasks?				
1. Feeding and watering	3	2	1	0
2. Weeding	3	2	1	0
3. Grooming pets	3	2	1	0
4. Breeding pets	3	2	1	0
5. Tree trimming	3	2	1	0
6. Planting	3	2	1	0
7. Gardening	3	2	1	0
8. Training pets	3	2	1	0
9. Landscaping	3	2	1	0
10. Farming	3	2	1	0

Section 1 Total: _____

	Very Skilled	Somewhat Skilled	Poorly Skilled	Not skilled or N/A
In working with your hands, how skilled are you at the following tasks?				
11. Building	3	2	1	0
12. Wiring	3	2	1	0
13. Remodeling	3	2	1	0
14. Repairing	3	2	1	0
15. Plumbing	3	2	1	0
16. Wallpapering	3	2	1	0
17. Measuring	3	2	1	0
18. Designing buildings	3	2	1	0
19. Drafting	3	2	1	0
20. Using tools	3	2	1	0

Section 2 Total: _____

	Very Skilled	Somewhat Skilled	Poorly Skilled	Not skilled or N/A
In expressing your ideas creatively, how skilled are you at the following tasks?				
21. Singing	3	2	1	0
22. Dancing	3	2	1	0
23. Taking photographs	3	2	1	0
24. Drawing	3	2	1	0
25. Writing	3	2	1	0
26. Performing	3	2	1	0
27. Editing	3	2	1	0
28. Designing	3	2	1	0
29. Painting	3	2	1	0
30. Sculpting	3	2	1	0

Section 3 Total: _____

	Very Skilled	Somewhat Skilled	Poorly Skilled	Not skilled or N/A
In working with others to complete projects, how skilled are you at the following tasks?				
31. Supervising	3	2	1	0
32. Coordinating events	3	2	1	0
33. Planning	3	2	1	0
34. Organizing	3	2	1	0
35. Directing	3	2	1	0
36. Delegating	3	2	1	0
37. Managing	3	2	1	0
38. Bookkeeping	3	2	1	0
39. Filing	3	2	1	0
40. Discharging employees	3	2	1	0

Section 4 Total: _____

In helping people to learn, how skilled are you at the following tasks?				
41. Tutoring	3	2	1	0
42. Coaching	3	2	1	0
43. Teaching	3	2	1	0
44. Training	3	2	1	0
45. Planning lessons	3	2	1	0
46. Encouraging	3	2	1	0
47. Counseling	3	2	1	0
48. Mentoring	3	2	1	0
49. Testing knowledge	3	2	1	0
50. Explaining ideas	3	2	1	0

Section 5 Total: _____

In making decisions involving money, how skilled are you at the following tasks?				
51. Accounting	3	2	1	0
52. Budgeting	3	2	1	0
53. Calculating	3	2	1	0
54. Analyzing data	3	2	1	0
55. Managing inventory	3	2	1	0
56. Auditing	3	2	1	0
57. Financial planning	3	2	1	0
58. Selling	3	2	1	0

(continued)

(continued)

	Very Skilled	Somewhat Skilled	Poorly Skilled	Not skilled or N/A
59. Investing	3	2	1	0
60. Solving math problems	3	2	1	0

Section 6 Total: _____

In helping an organization, how skilled are you at the following tasks?

	Very Skilled	Somewhat Skilled	Poorly Skilled	Not skilled or N/A
61. Campaigning	3	2	1	0
62. Lobbying	3	2	1	0
63. Inspecting	3	2	1	0
64. Planning	3	2	1	0
65. Reporting	3	2	1	0
66. Proofreading	3	2	1	0
67. Compiling statistics	3	2	1	0
68. Entering data	3	2	1	0
69. Keeping records	3	2	1	0
70. Evaluating	3	2	1	0

Section 7 Total: _____

In helping people be healthier, how skilled are you at the following tasks?

	Very Skilled	Somewhat Skilled	Poorly Skilled	Not skilled or N/A
71. Caring for others	3	2	1	0
72. Nursing	3	2	1	0
73. Treating injuries	3	2	1	0
74. Doing research	3	2	1	0
75. Examining specimens	3	2	1	0
76. Diagnosing	3	2	1	0
77. Performing experiments	3	2	1	0
78. Healing	3	2	1	0
79. Fixing teeth	3	2	1	0
80. Dispensing medicines	3	2	1	0

Section 8 Total: _____

In helping to meet other people's needs, how skilled are you at the following tasks?

	Very Skilled	Somewhat Skilled	Poorly Skilled	Not skilled or N/A
81. Coaching sports	3	2	1	0
82. Entertaining	3	2	1	0
83. Cooking/baking	3	2	1	0
84. Serving others	3	2	1	0
85. Playing sports	3	2	1	0
86. Cleaning	3	2	1	0

	Very Skilled	Somewhat Skilled	Poorly Skilled	Not skilled or N/A
87. Nurturing	3	2	1	0
88. Guiding tours	3	2	1	0
89. Planning events	3	2	1	0
90. Traveling	3	2	1	0

Section 9 Total: _____

In helping other people improve their overall well-being, how skilled are you at the following tasks?

91. Counseling	3	2	1	0
92. Monitoring client progress	3	2	1	0
93. Empathizing	3	2	1	0
94. Solving problems	3	2	1	0
95. Mentoring	3	2	1	0
96. Helping people with disabilities	3	2	1	0
97. Camp counseling	3	2	1	0
98. Facilitating groups	3	2	1	0
99. Listening	3	2	1	0
100. Studying behavior	3	2	1	0

Section 10 Total: _____

In working with computers, how skilled are you at the following tasks?

101. Programming computers	3	2	1	0
102. Creating web pages	3	2	1	0
103. Repairing computers	3	2	1	0
104. Analyzing systems	3	2	1	0
105. Analyzing data	3	2	1	0
106. Technical writing	3	2	1	0
107. Designing software	3	2	1	0
108. Applying software	3	2	1	0
109. Maintaining networks	3	2	1	0
110. Securing networks	3	2	1	0

Section 11 Total: _____

In protecting others, how skilled are you at the following tasks?

111. Doing research	3	2	1	0
112. Rehabilitating people	3	2	1	0
113. Enforcing regulations	3	2	1	0
114. Investigating	3	2	1	0

(continued)

(continued)

	Very Skilled	Somewhat Skilled	Poorly Skilled	Not skilled or N/A
115. Guarding	3	2	1	0
116. Inspecting	3	2	1	0
117. Fighting fires	3	2	1	0
118. Defending	3	2	1	0
119. Handling firearms	3	2	1	0
120. Debating	3	2	1	0

Section 12 Total: _____

In using machines, how skilled are you at the following tasks?

	Very Skilled	Somewhat Skilled	Poorly Skilled	Not skilled or N/A
121. Repairing	3	2	1	0
122. Assembling	3	2	1	0
123. Installing	3	2	1	0
124. Maintaining	3	2	1	0
125. Setting up	3	2	1	0
126. Drilling	3	2	1	0
127. Welding	3	2	1	0
128. Grinding	3	2	1	0
129. Forging	3	2	1	0
130. Operating	3	2	1	0

Section 13 Total: _____

In persuading others, how skilled are you at the following tasks?

	Very Skilled	Somewhat Skilled	Poorly Skilled	Not skilled or N/A
131. Marketing	3	2	1	0
132. Influencing	3	2	1	0
133. Promoting products	3	2	1	0
134. Selling	3	2	1	0
135. Demonstrating	3	2	1	0
136. Raising money	3	2	1	0
137. Writing proposals	3	2	1	0
138. Publicizing	3	2	1	0
139. Speaking publicly	3	2	1	0
140. Communicating	3	2	1	0

Section 14 Total: _____

In working with the sciences, how skilled are you at the following tasks?

	Very Skilled	Somewhat Skilled	Poorly Skilled	Not skilled or N/A
141. Teaching	3	2	1	0
142. Inventing	3	2	1	0

	Very Skilled	Somewhat Skilled	Poorly Skilled	Not skilled or N/A
143. Discovering	3	2	1	0
144. Hypothesizing	3	2	1	0
145. Conceptualizing	3	2	1	0
146. Formulating	3	2	1	0
147. Reviewing data	3	2	1	0
148. Conducting experiments	3	2	1	0
149. Researching	3	2	1	0
150. Systematizing data	3	2	1	0

Section 15 Total: _____

In moving people or materials, how skilled are you at the following tasks?

	Very Skilled	Somewhat Skilled	Poorly Skilled	Not skilled or N/A
151. Estimating distances	3	2	1	0
152. Pushing clutches	3	2	1	0
153. Driving	3	2	1	0
154. Operating machinery	3	2	1	0
155. Piloting boats	3	2	1	0
156. Navigating ships	3	2	1	0
157. Shipping	3	2	1	0
158. Unloading	3	2	1	0
159. Flying	3	2	1	0
160. Delivering	3	2	1	0

Section 16 Total: _____

Scoring

The Career Skills Inventory is made up of 16 sections representing the same 16 major career clusters as the Career Interest Inventory in Chapter 4. For each of the 16 sections on the previous pages, add the numbers you circled for each item. Put that total on the line at the end of each section. The higher the total number for each section, the more skilled you are in that particular career cluster. For each section, a score from 0 to 10 is low, a score from 11 to 20 is average, and a score from 21 to 30 is high.

Matching Your Skills to Careers

For each of the 16 areas that follow, list your score on the Career Skills Inventory and whether it was low, average, or high.

1. **Agriculture and Natural Resources:** Working with plants, animals, forests, or mineral resources for agriculture, horticulture, conservation, and other purposes.

   Skill: _____

2. **Architecture and Construction:** Designing, assembling, and maintaining buildings and other structures.

   Skill: _____

3. **Arts and Communication:** Creatively expressing feelings or ideas, communicating news or information, or performing.

   Skill: _____

4. **Business and Administration:** Making an organization run smoothly.

   Skill: _____

5. **Education and Training:** Helping people learn.

   Skill: _____

6. **Finance and Insurance:** Helping businesses and people secure their financial future.

   Skill: _____

7. **Government and Public Administration:** Helping a government agency serve the needs of the public.

   Skill: _____

8. **Health Science:** Keeping people and animals healthy.

   Skill: _____

9. **Hospitality, Tourism, and Recreation:** Catering to the wishes and needs of others so that they may enjoy a clean environment, good food and drink, comfortable accommodations, and recreation.

   Skill: _____

10. **Human Service:** Improving people's social, mental, emotional, or spiritual well-being.

    Skill: _____

11. **Information Technology:** Designing, developing, managing, and supporting information systems.

    Skill: _____

12. **Law and Public Safety:** Upholding people's rights or protecting people and property.

    Skill: _____

13. **Manufacturing:** Processing materials into products or maintaining and repairing products by using machines or hand tools.

   Skill: _____

14. **Retail and Wholesale Sales and Service:** Bringing others to a particular point of view through personal persuasion and sales techniques.

   Skill: _____

15. **Scientific Research, Engineering, and Mathematics:** Discovering, collecting, and analyzing information about the natural world, life sciences, and human behavior.

   Skill: _____

16. **Transportation, Distribution, and Logistics:** Moving people or materials.

   Skill: _____

IDENTIFYING THE FIVE CAREER CLUSTERS THAT BEST FIT YOUR SKILLS

Looking back over your results, which of the 16 career clusters yielded the highest total scores? Use the following space to list the five career clusters you scored highest in. This provides an excellent clue as to the kind of major you will find the most satisfaction in (and will probably be good at).

1. _____

2. _____

3. _____

4. _____

5. _____

Take a look at the list you made at the end of Chapter 4 of the five career clusters you are most interested in. How does this list relate to this list you just made of the five career clusters that best fit your skills? Keep in mind that you may have a high interest level in a certain career cluster, but a low skill level. (The opposite also can be true.) Of course, just because you don't have the skills related to a particular career doesn't mean you shouldn't pursue it—skills can be learned, after all. You should, however, begin your college major exploration with career clusters in which you have both a high interest level and a high skill level.

All people have a wide variety of skills, and you are no different. Many believe that skills and skills identification have the most important impact on your success in a chosen major. Everyone can learn and improve skills, but the most successful people are able to identify the skills that come naturally. This chapter was designed to help you explore and identify the skills that you bring to the workplace and specific occupations. Some of the skills you identified by completing the quiz in this chapter you were probably keenly aware of; other skills you may have been quite unaware of. The next chapter will continue the career exploration process by asking you to identify your favorite subjects while you were in high school.

Examine Your Favorite Subjects

The subjects you enjoy the most are an important indicator of what you might like to study in college. Think about the areas of study that you most enjoyed and least enjoyed. For example, Karen most enjoyed her high school classes that were science and math based, such as biology, chemistry, and geometry. She thinks that she might like to major in biology in college and eventually go on to pharmacy school when she completes her bachelor's degree. On the other hand, Jason enjoyed the creative arts when he was in high school. He liked his English classes, anything that involved writing, and theatre. He also acted in a few plays during the course of his time in high school. He says he wants to major in journalism with a minor in theatre. Some day after college, he hopes to write for a newspaper and maybe be a film critic.

Much like Karen and Jason, by thinking about the classes you have liked (and disliked), you will discover talents and strengths you never realized you had. For example, you may have had an art class in high school in which you learned about photography and were allowed to work in the school's darkroom to develop pictures. By taking this course, you may have realized that you have a passion for taking photographs, but you don't know if you could make a living by taking photographs. You also may have taken an English class in which you discovered that you have a talent for writing stories. By putting the two together, you may decide that a major in journalism and a minor in photography with a career in photojournalism might be a great long-term goal.

Although this process may seem lengthy, each time you reflect on your various passions from the past, you will continue to clarify who you are and what you want to do in life. The more you know about yourself, the more able you are to focus on those areas that make use of your natural interests. Take a look at the courses you enjoyed in high school for clues. While you were attending high

school, you probably got the best grades in the courses that allowed you to use your natural talents and passions. This will not change for you in college. The more you enjoy something, the more motivated you will be to study it and apply it in an occupation. The quiz in this chapter will help you connect your past academic experiences to a current college major and future career.

The Favorite Subjects Scale

Your favorite subjects in high school are a prime indicator of what you might like to study while in college. This quiz will help you identify the subjects you might like in the future by looking back at the subjects you enjoyed most in the past.

Read each statement carefully. Using the following scale, circle the number of the response that shows how descriptive each statement is of you:

3 = Liked a Lot

2 = Liked a Little

1 = Did Not Like

0 = Did Not Take

Please respond to every subject listed. Remember that there are no right or wrong answers.

In high school, I enjoyed...	Liked a Lot	Liked a Little	Did Not Like	Did Not Take
1. Animal Science	3	2	1	0
2. Environmental Science	3	2	1	0
3. Food Science	3	2	1	0
4. Horticulture	3	2	1	0
5. Physical Science	3	2	1	0
6. Zoology	3	2	1	0
7. Forestry	3	2	1	0
8. Physics	3	2	1	0
9. Soil Science	3	2	1	0
10. Earth Science	3	2	1	0

Section 1 Total: _____

In high school, I enjoyed...				
11. Art	3	2	1	0
12. Drafting	3	2	1	0

	Liked a Lot	Liked a Little	Did Not Like	Did Not Take
13. Computerized Drafting	3	2	1	0
14. Electronics	3	2	1	0
15. Industrial Arts	3	2	1	0
16. Mechanics	3	2	1	0
17. Wood Shop	3	2	1	0
18. Masonry	3	2	1	0
19. Electricity	3	2	1	0
20. Construction Technology	3	2	1	0

Section 2 Total: _____3_____

In high school, I enjoyed…

	Liked a Lot	Liked a Little	Did Not Like	Did Not Take
21. Fine Arts	3	2	1	0
22. Music	3	2	1	0
23. Public Speaking	3	2	1	0
24. Writing	3	2	1	0
25. English	3	2	1	0
26. Theatre	3	2	1	0
27. Choir	3	2	1	0
28. Graphic Design	3	2	1	0
29. Photography	3	2	1	0
30. Drafting	3	2	1	0

Section 3 Total: _____18_____

In high school, I enjoyed…

	Liked a Lot	Liked a Little	Did Not Like	Did Not Take
31. Accounting	3	2	1	0
32. Business Math	3	2	1	0
33. Business Writing	3	2	1	0
34. Economics	3	2	1	0
35. Finance	3	2	1	0
36. Marketing	3	2	1	0
37. Business Communication	3	2	1	0
38. Leadership	3	2	1	0
39. Business Law	3	2	1	0
40. Entrepreneurship	3	2	1	0

Section 4 Total: _____3_____

(continued)

(continued)

In high school, I enjoyed...	Liked a Lot	Liked a Little	Did Not Like	Did Not Take
41. Foreign Languages	(3)	2	1	0
42. History	(3)	2	1	0
43. Human Growth and Development	(3)	2	1	0
44. Public Speaking	(3)	2	1	0
45. Literature	(3)	2	1	0
46. Psychology	3	2	1	(0)
47. Physical Education	(3)	2	1	0
48. English Composition	3	2	1	(0)
49. Computer Technology	3	2	1	(0)
50. Math	3 20	(2)	1	0

Section 5 Total: _____

In high school, I enjoyed...	Liked a Lot	Liked a Little	Did Not Like	Did Not Take
51. Accounting	3	2	1	(0)
52. Finance	3	2	1	(0)
53. Statistics	3	(2)	1	0
54. Economics	3	2	1	(0)
55. Personal Finance	3	2	1	(0)
56. Political Science	3	2	1	(0)
57. Business	3	2	1	0
58. Marketing	3	2	1	0
59. Consumer Behavior	3	2	1	0
60. Psychology	3 2	2	1	0

Section 6 Total: _____

In high school, I enjoyed...	Liked a Lot	Liked a Little	Did Not Like	Did Not Take
61. Office Administration	3	2	1	(0)
62. Bookkeeping	3	2	1	(0)
63. Sociology	3	2	1	(0)
64. Research and Statistics	3	2	1	0
65. Computer Systems Technology	3	2	1	0
66. Clerical/Office Practices	3	2	1	0
67. Public Speaking	3	2	1	0
68. Database Management	3	2	1	0

	Liked a Lot	Liked a Little	Did Not Like	Did Not Take
69. Political Science	3	2	1	0
70. Network Administration	3	2	1	0

Section 7 Total: _3_

In high school, I enjoyed…

	Liked a Lot	Liked a Little	Did Not Like	Did Not Take
71. Athletics	3	2	1	0
72. Health Education	3	2	1	0
73. Physical Education	3	2	1	0
74. Anatomy	3	2	1	0
75. Chemistry	3	2	1	0
76. Genetics	3	2	1	0
77. Physics	3	2	1	0
78. Nursing	3	2	1	0
79. Biology	3	2	1	0
80. Medical Science	3	2	1	0

Section 8 Total: _2_

In high school, I enjoyed…

	Liked a Lot	Liked a Little	Did Not Like	Did Not Take
81. Cosmetology	(3)	2	1	0
82. Physical Education	3	2	1	0
83. Culinary Arts	(3)	2	1	0
84. Home Economics	3	2	1	0
85. Consumer Education	3	2	1	0
86. Health	(3)	2	1	0
87. Hospitality Management	3	2	1	0
88. Sports Studies	3	2	1	0
89. Recreation Management	3	2	1	0
90. Fashion Design	(3)	2	1	0

Section 9 Total: _12_

In high school, I enjoyed…

	Liked a Lot	Liked a Little	Did Not Like	Did Not Take
91. Psychology	3	2	1	0
92. Child Development	3	2	1	0
93. Philosophy	3	2	1	0
94. Sociology	3	2	1	0
95. Religious Studies	3	2	1	0
96. Public Speaking	3	2	1	0

(continued)

(continued)

	Liked a Lot	Liked a Little	Did Not Like	Did Not Take
97. Social Problems	3	2	1	0
98. Social Studies	3	2	1	0
99. History	3	2	1	0
100. Criminal Justice	⌐3	2	1	0

Section 10 Total: _____

In high school, I enjoyed…

101. Calculus	3	2	1	0
102. Network Management	3	2	1	0
103. Computer Science	3	2	1	0
104. Graphic Design	3	2	1	0
105. Robotics	3	2	1	0
106. Technical Writing	3	2	1	0
107. Web Page Development	3	2	1	0
108. Information Systems	3	2	1	0
109. Computer Programming	3	2	1	0
110. Database Management	3	2	1	0

Section 11 Total: _____

In high school, I enjoyed…

111. Criminal Justice	3	2	1	0
112. Sociology	3	2	1	0
113. Political Science	3	2	1	0
114. Law	3	2	1	0
115. Philosophy	3	2	1	0
116. Science	3	2	1	0
117. Business Law	3	2	1	0
118. Public Speaking	3	2	1	0
119. Foreign Languages	3	2	1	0
120. Military Science	3	2	1	0

Section 12 Total: _____

In high school, I enjoyed…

121. Mechanics	3	2	1	0
122. Automotive Repair	3	2	1	0
123. Industrial Arts	3	2	1	0
124. Print Shop	3	2	1	0

	Liked a Lot	Liked a Little	Did Not Like	Did Not Take
125. Welding	3	2	1	0
126. Machine Shop	3	2	1	0
127. Electronics	3	2	1	0
128. Wood Shop	3	2	1	0
129. Metal Shop	3	2	1	0
130. Photography	3	2	1	0

Section 13 Total: _____

In high school, I enjoyed...

	Liked a Lot	Liked a Little	Did Not Like	Did Not Take
131. Public Speaking	3	2	1	0
132. Consumer Behavior	3	2	1	0
133. Marketing	3	2	1	0
134. Business	3	2	1	0
135. Merchandising	3	2	1	0
136. Advertising	3	2	1	0
137. Art	3	2	1	0
138. Writing	3	2	1	0
139. Psychology	3	2	1	0
140. Photography	3	2	1	0

Section 14 Total: _____

In high school, I enjoyed...

	Liked a Lot	Liked a Little	Did Not Like	Did Not Take
141. Science	3	2	1	0
142. History	3	2	1	0
143. Math	3	2	1	0
144. Astronomy	3	2	1	0
145. Research and Statistics	3	2	1	0
146. Geography	3	2	1	0
147. Chemistry	3	2	1	0
148. Earth Science	3	2	1	0
149. Economics	3	2	1	0
150. Anthropology	3	2	1	0

Section 15 Total: _____

In high school, I enjoyed...

	Liked a Lot	Liked a Little	Did Not Like	Did Not Take
151. Driver Education	3	2	1	0
152. Industrial Arts	3	2	1	0

(continued)

(continued)

	Liked a Lot	Liked a Little	Did Not Like	Did Not Take
153. Automotive Technology	3	2	1	0
154. Machine Technology	3	2	1	0
155. Aviation	3	2	1	0
156. Science	3	2	1	0
157. Transportation Systems	3	2	1	0
158. Urban Studies	3	2	1	0
159. Transportation Planning	3	2	1	0
160. Transportation Technology	3	2	1	0
Section 16 Total: _____				

Scoring

The inventory you just completed will help you identify the subjects you enjoyed most in the past. For each of the sections on the previous pages, add the scores you circled for each of the sections. Put that total on the line marked "Total" at the end of each section. Your score in each section can range from 0 to 30, with a score of 0 to 10 indicating a low level of enjoyment or experience in that area, 11 to 20 indicating an average level of enjoyment or experience in that area, and a score of 21 to 30 indicating a high level of enjoyment or experience in that area.

Matching Your Favorite Subjects to Careers

Occupational information is often organized by using career clusters. The assessment you just took is organized around the United States Department of Education career clusters. For each of the 16 areas that follow, list your score on the Favorite Subjects Scale and whether it was low, average, or high. Note that the numbers of the clusters match the numbers of the sections in the Favorite Subjects Scale.

1. **Agriculture and Natural Resources:** Subjects relating to working with plants, animals, or mineral resources for agriculture, horticulture, conservation, and other purposes.

   Subject enjoyment: _____

2. **Architecture and Construction:** Subjects relating to designing, assembling, and maintaining buildings and other structures.

   Subject enjoyment: _____

3. **Arts and Communication:** Subjects relating to creatively expressing feelings or ideas, communicating news or information, or performing.

   Subject enjoyment: _____

4. **Business and Administration:** Subjects relating to making an organization run smoothly.

   Subject enjoyment: _____

5. **Education and Training:** Subjects relating to helping people learn.

   Subject enjoyment: _____

6. **Finance and Insurance:** Subjects relating to helping businesses and people secure their financial future.

   Subject enjoyment: _____

7. **Government and Public Administration:** Subjects relating to helping government agencies serve the needs of the public.

   Subject enjoyment: _____

8. **Health Science:** Subjects relating to helping people and animals be healthy.

   Subject enjoyment: _____

9. **Hospitality, Tourism, and Recreation:** Subjects relating to catering to the wishes and needs of others so that they may enjoy a clean environment, good food and drink, comfortable accommodations, and recreation.

   Subject enjoyment: _____

10. **Human Service:** Subjects relating to improving people's social, mental, emotional, or spiritual well-being.

    Subject enjoyment: _____

11. **Information Technology:** Subjects relating to designing, developing, managing, and supporting information systems.

    Subject enjoyment: _____

12. **Law and Public Safety:** Subjects relating to upholding people's rights or protecting people and property.

    Subject enjoyment: _____

13. **Manufacturing:** Subjects relating to processing materials into products or maintaining and repairing products by using machines or hand tools.

    Subject enjoyment: _____

14. **Retail and Wholesale Sales and Service:** Subjects relating to bringing others to a particular point of view through personal persuasion and sales techniques.

    Subject enjoyment: _____

15. **Scientific Research, Engineering, and Mathematics:** Subjects relating to discovering, collecting, and analyzing information about the natural world, life sciences, and human behavior.

    Subject enjoyment: _____

16. **Transportation, Distribution, and Logistics:** Subjects relating to operations that move people or materials.

    Subject enjoyment: _____

CONNECTING CAREER CLUSTERS TO YOUR FAVORITE SUBJECTS

Looking back over your results, which of the 16 career clusters yielded the highest total score? Use the following space to list the five career clusters you scored highest in. This list provides an excellent clue as to the kind of major you will find the most satisfaction in (and will probably be good at)

1. _____

2. _____

3. _____

4. _____

5. _____

From Subjects to Clusters to Careers

The following table shows a sampling of career options for each of the 16 clusters. Starting with the five clusters you listed in the previous worksheet, read through the list of job titles, checking any that sound interesting to you. Do not worry about the amount of education and training required for these jobs. For now, just isolate potential careers that you would consider pursuing.

Agriculture and Natural Resources

- ☐ Agricultural Engineer
- ☐ Animal Scientist
- ☐ Conservation Scientist
- ☐ Conservation Worker
- ☐ Environmental Engineer
- ☐ Farm Manager
- ☐ Fish Hatchery Manager
- ☐ Food Scientist
- ☐ Forester
- ☐ Geological Data Technician
- ☐ Land Use Planner
- ☐ Nursery and Greenhouse Manager
- ☐ Park Naturalist
- ☐ Pest Control Worker
- ☐ Petroleum Engineer
- ☐ Soil Conservationist
- ☐ Soil Scientist
- ☐ Wildlife Biologist
- ☐ Wildlife Technician
- ☐ Veterinarian
- ☐ Zoologist

Architecture and Construction

- ☐ Architect
- ☐ Architectural Drafter
- ☐ Brickmason
- ☐ Building Inspector
- ☐ Bulldozer Operator
- ☐ Ceiling Tile Installer
- ☐ City Planner
- ☐ Construction Inspector
- ☐ Construction Manager
- ☐ Crane Operator
- ☐ Drafter
- ☐ Drywall Installer
- ☐ Electrician
- ☐ Engineering Technician
- ☐ Geographic Specialist
- ☐ Heating and Air Conditioning Mechanic
- ☐ Home Appliance Installer
- ☐ Insulation Worker
- ☐ Paperhanger
- ☐ Pipelayer
- ☐ Plumber
- ☐ Roofer
- ☐ Stonemason
- ☐ Surveyor

Arts and Communication

- ☐ Actor
- ☐ Art Director
- ☐ Broadcast News Analyst
- ☐ Cartoonist

(continued)

(continued)

- ☐ Choreographer
- ☐ Composer
- ☐ Dancer
- ☐ Editor
- ☐ Fashion Designer
- ☐ Graphic Designer
- ☐ Interior Designer
- ☐ Interpreter or Translator
- ☐ Musician

- ☐ Painter
- ☐ Photographer
- ☐ Public Relations Manager
- ☐ Reporter
- ☐ Sculptor
- ☐ Radio and Television Announcer
- ☐ Sound Engineering Technician
- ☐ Writer

Business and Administration

- ☐ Accountant
- ☐ Administrative Assistant
- ☐ Auditors
- ☐ Brokerage Clerk
- ☐ Budget Analyst
- ☐ Chief Executive
- ☐ File Clerk
- ☐ Human Resources Manager
- ☐ Legal Secretary

- ☐ Management Analyst
- ☐ Medical Secretary
- ☐ Meeting and Convention Planner
- ☐ Office Clerk
- ☐ Personnel Recruiter
- ☐ Post Office Clerk
- ☐ Shipping Clerk
- ☐ Tax Preparer

Education and Training

- ☐ Adult Education Teacher
- ☐ Archivist
- ☐ Curator
- ☐ Educational Counselor
- ☐ Education Policy Analyst
- ☐ Elementary School Teacher
- ☐ Fitness Trainer
- ☐ Instructional Coordinator

- ☐ Kindergarten Teacher
- ☐ Librarian
- ☐ Library Assistant
- ☐ Middle School Teacher
- ☐ Museum Technician
- ☐ Postsecondary Teacher
- ☐ Preschool Teacher
- ☐ Secondary School Teacher

☐ Special Education Teacher

☐ Teacher Assistant

☐ Vocational Education Teacher

Finance and Insurance

☐ Advertising Sales Agent

☐ Appraiser

☐ Assessor

☐ Bank Teller

☐ Bill and Account Collector

☐ Cost Estimator

☐ Credit Checker

☐ Financial Analyst

☐ Financial Manager

☐ Insurance Adjuster

☐ Insurance Underwriter

☐ Loan Counselor

☐ Loan Officer

☐ Market Research Analyst

☐ Personal Financial Advisor

☐ Securities and Commodities Sales

☐ Survey Researcher

☐ Treasurer

Government and Public Administration

☐ Agricultural Inspector

☐ Aviation Inspector

☐ City Planning Aide

☐ Court Clerk

☐ Court Reporter

☐ Environmental Compliance Inspector

☐ Equal Opportunity Representative

☐ Financial Examiner

☐ Fire Inspector

☐ Fish and Game Warden

☐ Foreign Service Officer

☐ Government Property Inspector

☐ Immigration and Customs Inspector

☐ License Clerk

☐ Licensing Examiner

☐ Missing Persons Investigator

☐ Municipal Clerk

☐ Public Interest Advocate

☐ Urban Planner

☐ Tax Examiner or Collector

Health Science

☐ Anesthesiologist

☐ Athletic Trainer

☐ Audiologist

☐ Cardiovascular Technologist

☐ Chiropractor

☐ Coroner

☐ Dental Assistant or Hygienist

☐ Dentist

☐ Dietician or Nutritionist

☐ Home Health Aide

(continued)

(continued)

☐ Laboratory Technician

☐ Nurse

☐ Massage Therapist

☐ Medical Sonographer

☐ Medical Transcriptionist

☐ Occupational Therapist

☐ Optician

☐ Pediatrician

☐ Pharmacist

☐ Psychiatrist

☐ Radiologic Technologist

☐ Respiratory Therapist

☐ Surgeon

☐ Veterinarian

Hospitality, Tourism, and Recreation

☐ Amusement Attendant

☐ Baker

☐ Chef

☐ Concierge

☐ Cook

☐ Counter Attendant

☐ Flight Attendant

☐ Food Service Manager

☐ Gaming Dealer or Manager

☐ Hairdresser

☐ Home Care Aide

☐ Hospitality Administrator

☐ Hotel Desk Clerk

☐ Hotel Manager

☐ Lodging Manager

☐ Mortician

☐ Outdoor Education Specialist

☐ Recreation Therapist

☐ Recreation Worker

☐ Ticket Agent

☐ Tour Guide

☐ Travel Agent

Human Service

☐ Child Care Worker

☐ Clergy

☐ Clinical Psychologist

☐ Correctional Treatment Specialist

☐ Counselor

☐ Funeral Attendant

☐ Interviewer

☐ Marriage and Family Therapist

☐ Mental Health Counselor

☐ Personal and Home Care Aide

☐ Probation Officer

☐ Rehabilitation Counselor

☐ Residential Advisor

☐ Social and Human Services Assistant

☐ Social Worker

Information Technology

- ☐ Computer and Information Systems Manager
- ☐ Computer Operator
- ☐ Computer Programmer
- ☐ Computer Scientist
- ☐ Computer Security Specialist
- ☐ Computer Software Engineer
- ☐ Computer Systems Analyst
- ☐ Database Administrator
- ☐ Data Processing Equipment Repairer
- ☐ Network Administrator
- ☐ Office Machine Repairer
- ☐ Web Developer

Law and Public Safety

- ☐ Arbitrator
- ☐ Bailiff
- ☐ Correctional Officer
- ☐ Criminal Investigator
- ☐ Emergency Medical Technician or Paramedic
- ☐ Firefighter
- ☐ Fire Investigator
- ☐ Highway Patroller
- ☐ Judge
- ☐ Law Clerk
- ☐ Lawyer
- ☐ Mediator
- ☐ Paralegal
- ☐ Police Detective
- ☐ Private Detective
- ☐ Security Guard
- ☐ Sheriff or Deputy Sheriff
- ☐ Title Searcher

Manufacturing

- ☐ Aircraft Engine Specialist
- ☐ Appliance Repairer
- ☐ Automotive Specialty Technician
- ☐ Bookbinder
- ☐ Cabinetmaker
- ☐ Computer Control Operator
- ☐ Dental Lab Technician
- ☐ Industrial Production Manager
- ☐ Jeweler
- ☐ Machinist
- ☐ Molding and Casting Worker
- ☐ Power Plant Operator
- ☐ Printing Machine Operator
- ☐ Production Laborer
- ☐ Semiconductor Processor
- ☐ Soldering Machine Operator
- ☐ Stationary Engineer
- ☐ Tool and Die Maker

Retail and Wholesale Sales and Service

☐ Adjustment Clerk
☐ Advertising Manager
☐ Buyer
☐ Counter and Rental Clerk
☐ Customer Service Representative
☐ Demonstrator
☐ Funeral Director
☐ Marketing Manager
☐ Model

☐ Purchasing Agent
☐ Purchasing Manager
☐ Real Estate Broker
☐ Receptionist and Information Clerk
☐ Retail Salesperson
☐ Sales Engineer
☐ Sales Representative
☐ Sales Manager

Scientific Research, Engineering, and Mathematics

☐ Actuary
☐ Anthropologist
☐ Archeologist
☐ Astronomer
☐ Biologist
☐ Chemist
☐ Chemical Engineer
☐ Economist
☐ Epidemiologist

☐ Geographer
☐ Educational Psychologist
☐ Materials Scientist
☐ Materials Engineer
☐ Mechanical Engineer
☐ Meteorologist
☐ Physicist
☐ Sociologist
☐ Statistician

Transportation, Distribution, and Logistics

☐ Air Traffic Controller
☐ Aircraft and Avionics Technician
☐ Airline Pilot or Flight Engineer
☐ Ambulance Driver
☐ Cargo and Freight Agent
☐ Courier
☐ Diesel Technician
☐ Driving Instructor

☐ Freight Inspector
☐ Heavy Equipment Technician
☐ Industrial Machinery Repairer
☐ Locomotive Engineer
☐ Postal Service Mail Carrier
☐ Public Transportation Inspector
☐ Subway and Streetcar Operator
☐ Traffic Technician

CHOOSING POTENTIAL CAREERS

Of all the occupations you just circled, which seem the most interesting to you? List the six occupations you would most like to explore in more detail:

1. _____

2. _____

3. _____

4. _____

5. _____

6. _____

High school subjects you enjoyed in the past can be an excellent predictor of majors you will enjoy in the future. Many college students will choose a major based solely on their interests in various high school subjects. Although this approach works for some people, it can be deceiving because you may not have been exposed to a wide enough variety of classes in high school. Therefore, you should use the information you learned in this chapter in conjunction with the information you learned in previous chapters, as well as the information you discover about yourself in the next chapter, which helps you identify your prominent personality traits.

PART 3: GET TO KNOW YOURSELF BETTER

"You have to know exactly what you want out of your career. If you want to be a star, you don't bother with other things."

—Marilyn Horne

Explore Your Personality

Kendra loves being with and taking care of animals. She has several pets of her own and often takes care of her neighbors' pets when the neighbors travel. She enjoys walking dogs and volunteers regularly at the animal shelter.

Joshua is an inquisitive person who enjoys solving problems that require him to do a lot of researching and investigating. He likes to be challenged intellectually and to debate ideas and beliefs with other people.

Although Shelley can be temperamental, she also is creative and imaginative, expressing herself through writing short stories. She does her best work in unstructured environments.

Peter volunteers for many organizations. A compassionate and caring person, he is always looking for ways to help people in need and make the world a better place.

A natural-born leader, Kathy is energetic, ambitious, and persuasive. She loves being in charge and directing and supervising other people.

Neat, organized, and precise, Shane is a master of detail. He prides himself on his accuracy in handling numbers and other information and his ability to spot inconsistencies in data. He feels most comfortable working in an office environment.

These are students with whom I have worked over the years. They all found a major through which they could express their unique personalities. One or several of them probably seem similar to you. The idea behind this chapter is simple: The greater the match is between your personality and college major, the greater life and career satisfaction you will have.

Your Unique Personality

Your personality affects your career development in a variety of ways. Knowing your personality helps you to understand:

- How you approach career decisions such as choosing a major

- How comfortable you will feel in certain majors

- How you interact with coworkers

- How you interact with other students in the major

- How well you like the coursework required in the major

- How you define your strengths and weaknesses

- How you recognize and value diversity in others

- How you solve problems and resolve conflicts

But before you can apply what you know about your personality to your decision about a college major, you have to have a good sense of what a personality is and how it develops.

What Are the Basic Elements of Personality?

Over the years, psychologists and spouses (but mainly psychologists) have proposed many different definitions of personality. Although these definitions often vary in the particulars, they share a few common elements:

- **Organization and consistency:** Different aspects of your personality are often linked together and guide your behavior in an organized and consistent way.

- **Physiological and psychological nature:** Your personality is influenced by your inherited traits and environmental conditions

- **Behavior motivation:** Your personality motivates you to behave in certain ways.

- **Connection to thoughts, actions, feelings, and interactions:** Personality is demonstrated through your thoughts, actions, feelings, and interactions with other people. Thus, you can identify the personality traits of others by observing how they think, feel, act, and interact.

How Does Personality Develop?

Although psychologists and other theorists generally agree that such a thing as personality exists, they disagree about how personality develops. Some theorists believe that personality is innate (part of our *nature*) and cannot easily be changed. They think that personality traits are inherited much like hair and eye color and that these traits determine the way the brain develops and how personality expresses itself. These personality traits reveal themselves early in life and remain constant throughout childhood and into adulthood.

On the other hand, some personality theorists believe that personality is primarily learned from our interactions early in life. Our personality traits are *nurtured* from our environment rather than embedded in our genes. These theorists believe that people are self-organizing, proactive, self-reflecting, and self-regulating rather than simply reactive organisms shaped by environmental forces or childhood circumstances.

Today, most experts on the subject of personality believe that your personality is a unique combination of heredity and environment. According to this theory, you can have a genetic predisposition to act in a certain way, but these behaviors are enhanced or replaced with more dominant personality traits acquired through interaction with the environment.

In conclusion, your personality can be seen as consistent styles of behavior and emotional reactions that are present from infancy onward and that develop as a result of a combination of heredity and early environmental experiences.

The Career Personality Inventory

Your career personality determines such things as whether you enjoy working indoors or outdoors, interacting with people or with information, making money or art (though those two don't *have* to be exclusive). The Career Personality Inventory (CPI) can help you identify your career personality and the core career and life themes associated with it.

The Career Personality Inventory contains a series of words that describe various personality traits that you may or may not have. Read each of the words listed and decide whether the word describes you. If it *does* describe you, circle the word. If it *does not* describe you, do not circle the word; simply move to the next word.

Take your time responding, but be sure to respond to every word listed. This is not a test, so there are no right or wrong answers.

I consider myself to be...

Conforming	Humble	Athletic
Frank	Handy	Persistent
Genuine	Modest	Practical
Hard-headed	Natural	Shy
Honest	Mechanical	Outdoorsy
Stable	Self-reliant	Physical

Section 1 Total: _____

I consider myself to be...

Analytical	Independent	Modest
Cautious	Intellectual	Pessimistic
Complex	Introverted	Precise

(continued)

(continued)

Critical	Methodical	Rational
Curious	Logical	Reserved
Scientific	Scholarly	Self-controlled

Section 2 Total: _____

I consider myself to be...

Complicated	Imaginative	Creative
Individualistic	Innovative	Intuitive
Emotional	Impulsive	Nonconforming
Expressive	Independent	Open
Idealistic	Artsy	Original
Uncontrolled	Daydreamer	Unstructured

Section 3 Total: _____

I consider myself to be...

Convincing	Idealistic	Sociable
Cooperative	Empathetic	Sympathetic
Emotional	Patient	Tactful
Generous	Responsible	Understanding
Helpful	Caring	Warm
Humanistic	People-oriented	Cheerful

Section 4 Total: _____

I consider myself to be...

Acquisitive	Domineering	Optimistic
Adventurous	Energetic	Assertive
Bold	Extroverted	Popular
Ambitious	Impulsive	Self-confident
Attention-getting	Persuasive	Sociable
Aggressive	Charismatic	Goal-driven

Section 5 Total: _____

I consider myself to be...

Conforming	Inhibited	Persistent
Conscientious	Obedient	Practical
Careful	Orderly	Thrifty
Efficient	Unimaginative	Reserved
Structured	Precise	Detail-oriented
Scheduled	Dependable	Self-controlled

Section 6 Total: _____

Scoring

This assessment is designed to help you make an effective decision about a major based on your personality type. The personality types used are those defined by career researcher John Holland: Realistic, Investigative, Artistic, Social, Enterprising, and Conventional. Count the total number of items you circled for each section. You will have a number between 0 and 18. Put that total on the line marked "Total" at the bottom of each section and then transfer your totals to the space below:

Realistic (Section 1) Total: _____

Investigative (Section 2) Total: _____

Artistic (Section 3) Total: _____

Social (Section 4) Total: _____

Enterprising (Section 5) Total: _____

Conventional (Section 6) Total: _____

Generally, the higher your score for a certain type, the more characteristics you share with others of that personality type. Scores from 18 to 13 are considered high, 12 to 6 are average, and those 5 and below are considered low.

Identify the scale on which you scored the highest. This is your primary personality type. In the descriptions that follow, you should explore all of the majors listed for that scale, especially if your score on this scale is much higher than the rest. However, if you had high scores on two or more scales, you should explore majors listed under each type, starting with the scale on which you scored highest. Bear in mind that the majors listed under each scale represent only a sample of those that might be of interest to that personality type.

Understanding the Scales

Career psychologist John Holland theorized that your personality type is reflective of your preferences for interests and activities as well as personal characteristics. The activities in which you choose to engage are unique yet similar to those of many other people in the world. Thus, similar personality types tend to be interested in similar activities. For example, people with the Social personality type like being around other people and helping them solve their problems. On the other hand, people with the Conventional personality type enjoy working with numbers and data, usually in an office by themselves, with very little contact with people.

Each of the following descriptions represents "pure" types. You will probably see some parts of each description fitting you in different roles you play. You might be primarily Artistic, but also have some parts of your personality that are described in the Realistic and Investigative descriptions. Look that the following types and try to determine which one best describes you.

Realistic

People with a Realistic personality type value concrete and physical tasks and see themselves as having mechanical skills and lacking social skills. They have a preference for activities that include the use of tools, objects, machines, and animals. Their preferred work often involves concrete, physical tasks requiring mechanical skills, persistence, and movement. Careers of interest include aircraft mechanic, truck driver, barber, and bricklayer.

College majors that are typically a good fit for this personality type include the following. Check the ones that interest you:

☐ Anthropology   ☐ Construction Management

☐ Agriculture   ☐ Food Science

☐ Agronomy   ☐ Forestry

☐ Animal Sciences   ☐ Heating and Air Conditioning

☐ Archeology   ☐ Industrial Education

☐ Broadcast Production   ☐ Recreation Management

☐ Criminal Justice   ☐ Robotics

☐ Computer-Aided Drafting   ☐ Tourism

Investigative

People with an Investigative personality type want to solve intellectual, scientific, and mathematical problems. They see themselves as scholarly, analytic, critical, curious, introspective, and methodical. They prefer activities that include the investigation of physical, biological, and cultural phenomena. Their work settings may include a research laboratory, diagnostic medical case conference, or a work group of scientists or medical researchers. Careers of interest include computer programmer, clinical psychologist, architect, dentist, and mathematician.

College majors that are typically a good fit for this personality type include the following. Check the ones that interest you:

☐ Astronomy   ☐ Environmental Science

☐ Athletic Training   ☐ Geology

☐ Biology   ☐ Information Systems

☐ Botany   ☐ Marine Biology

☐ Biotechnology   ☐ Mathematics

☐ Chemistry   ☐ Nursing

☐ Computer Programming   ☐ Psychology

☐ Engineering   ☐ Zoology

Artistic

People with the Artistic personality type like creative projects in the form of painting, writing, drama, or other art forms. They see themselves as imaginative, expressive, original, and independent. They prefer free, unsystematized activities that include the manipulation of materials to create art forms or products. Careers of interest include painter, actor or actress, designer, musician, editor, and radio or television announcer.

College majors that are typically a good fit for this personality type include the following. Check the ones that interest you:

☐ Advertising	☐ Graphic Design
☐ Art	☐ Interior Design
☐ Creative Writing	☐ Journalism
☐ Dance	☐ Literature
☐ English	☐ Music
☐ Fashion Design	☐ Photography
☐ Film Studies	☐ Public Relations
☐ Foreign Languages	☐ Theatre

Social

People with the Social personality type enjoy activities that involve informing, training, developing, curing, or enlightening others. They see themselves as being understanding, liking to help others, and having teaching ability. They value social or ethical activities and are cooperative, insightful, persuasive, and sociable. Careers of interest include counselor, nurse, teacher, social worker, judge, and minister.

College majors that are typically a good fit for this personality type include the following. Check the ones that interest you:

☐ Behavioral Science	☐ Preschool Education
☐ Child Care Management	☐ Recreation Therapy
☐ Counseling	☐ Religious Studies
☐ Early Childhood Education	☐ Secondary Education
☐ Elementary Education	☐ Social Science
☐ Human Services	☐ Social Work
☐ Middle School Education	☐ Special Education
☐ Physical Education	☐ Speech Therapy

Enterprising

People with the Enterprising personality type value political and economic achievements and leadership. They enjoy activities that satisfy their personal need for control, recognition, and power. They see themselves as extroverted, happy, assertive, popular, and self-confident. They prefer activities that involve attaining organizational goals or economic gain. Careers of interest include politician, realtor, attorney, and salesperson.

College majors that are typically a good fit for this personality type include the following. Check the ones that interest you:

- ☐ Banking
- ☐ Business Administration
- ☐ E-commerce
- ☐ Economics
- ☐ Entrepreneurship
- ☐ Finance
- ☐ Hotel/Motel Management
- ☐ Human Resource Management

- ☐ Industrial Relations
- ☐ Insurance
- ☐ International Business
- ☐ Management
- ☐ Marketing
- ☐ Organizational Behavior
- ☐ Pre-Law
- ☐ Restaurant Management

Conventional

People with a Conventional personality type value systematic, concrete tasks, often involving verbal and mathematical data. They see themselves as orderly, conformist, and skilled in clerical and numerical tasks. They prefer activities that include the manipulation of data, such as keeping records, filing materials, reproducing materials, and processing data to attain organizational or economic goals. Careers of interest include accountant, banker, file clerk, computer operator, and receptionist.

College majors that are typically a good fit for this personality type include the following. Check the ones that interest you:

- ☐ Accounting
- ☐ Actuarial Science
- ☐ Banking
- ☐ Business Education
- ☐ City Planning
- ☐ Computer Repair
- ☐ Data Management
- ☐ Database Administrator

- ☐ Information Technology
- ☐ Library Science
- ☐ Materials Management
- ☐ Office Management
- ☐ Paralegal Studies
- ☐ Public Administration
- ☐ Transportation Logistics
- ☐ Urban Planning

HOLLAND'S PERSONALITY THEORY

John Holland has created one of the most enduring theories of career development and career counseling. He believes that individuals search for work environments that allow them to express their personalities, and that such work is more satisfying because it allows for that expression. For decades, career counselors have used Holland's theory and his personality model to match people with congruent occupations.

Holland's model works under the following principles:

1. In our culture, most people can be categorized as one of six types: Realistic, Investigative, Artistic, Social, Enterprising, and Conventional.

2. In our culture, most work environments can be categorized as one of six types: Realistic, Investigative, Artistic, Social, Enterprising, and Conventional.

3. Given these six personality types, people search for environments that let them exercise their skills and abilities, express their attitudes and values, and take on agreeable roles and problems.

4. Behavior is determined by an interaction between personality and environment.

The Connection Between Personality and Major

Your personality type has been influenced by both your early life experiences as well as your heredity. Therefore, your personality type has been maturing and developing since you were a child. By the time you reached your teen years, your personality type began to crystallize and become a part of who you are. The theory of career development that is the basis for the assessment in this chapter is based on the notion that all jobs, as well as college majors, have different characteristic traits that correspond to the characteristic personality traits in people. Therefore, the compatibility of your personality type determines what type of work you would enjoy and thus the type of major at which you might excel.

The basic idea is that when your personality type matches the duties required in an occupation, you will find career satisfaction. For example, people who are investigative and inquisitive would most likely find career satisfaction in majors such as biology and geology. Holland's research shows that people who enter majors compatible with their personality type tend to be satisfied in their subsequent work and find stability on the job. On the other hand, an artistic type will be extremely dissatisfied when majoring in or entering an occupation that is primarily conventional in nature, such as accounting. Research also shows that people who enter occupations that are not compatible with their personality type tend to report a tremendous amount of job dissatisfaction and tend to be unstable in their jobs.

MATCHING YOUR PERSONALITY TO COLLEGE MAJORS

People who succeed in specific college majors and within occupations have certain personality characteristics in common. Using your results from the Career Personality Inventory and the majors checklists, list the majors that match your personality and sound exciting to you.

Your highest scoring personality type:

_____

Matching majors of interest within that type:

_____

_____

Your second highest scoring personality type:

_____

Matching majors of interest within that type:

_____

_____

Your third highest scoring personality type:

_____

Matching majors of interest within that type:

_____

_____

EXAMINING MAJORS OF INTEREST

In the table that follows, list up to five majors that you are seriously considering, and then identify what you like about that major and what you do not like about it.

Major of Interest	What You Like About It	What You Don't Like About It
_____	_____	_____
	_____	_____
	_____	_____
	_____	_____
	_____	_____

Major of Interest	What You Like About It	What You Don't Like About It
_____	_____	_____
	_____	_____
	_____	_____
	_____	_____
	_____	_____
_____	_____	_____
	_____	_____
	_____	_____
	_____	_____
	_____	_____
_____	_____	_____
	_____	_____
	_____	_____
	_____	_____
	_____	_____
_____	_____	_____
	_____	_____
	_____	_____
	_____	_____
	_____	_____

Remember that no assessment can tell you who you should be or what major you should engage in. Assessments can't choose your career path, they can only help you to better define it. Knowing more about your personality can narrow down the number of majors you might be interested in pursuing. At the same time, it might reveal possible majors you hadn't thought of before. By matching your personality with potential college majors, you have significantly improved your chances of finding happiness in your chosen field. In the next chapter, you will have an opportunity to clarify your values, or that which is most important to you. Your values are guiding principles that define you as a person and influence all that you do in your life and your career.

CHAPTER 8

Identify What Is Important to You

L ike all people, you have a specific set of values that guide your behavior and influence the decisions you make. Values are those things that you give merit, usefulness, or worth in your life.
They are those things you feel are desirable and important.

In this chapter, you will take a quiz to help you identify your values. Through a thorough exploration of your values, you will be able to define a clear direction for your career, which will help you
in identifying a college major.

Understanding Your Values

Everyday we face a barrage of information that reflects conflicting and ill-defined value systems.
The fortunate among us know what our values are and are able to articulate them.

One of my students, Shauna, said that helping other people and leaving the planet a better place
when she is gone were the most important things for her. Another student, Jeffrey, said that
autonomy and being able to work by himself were the most important things. Joan wants to be in
charge. She said that as long as she is "calling the shots," she is happy.

As these students demonstrate, values differ from person to person. Values are often based on the
conditions of life that you would like to see a reality, as shown in the following statements.

- "I would like to see people be more creative."

- "I would like to see all people learn and use current technologies."

- "I would like to see everyone live healthier."

- "I would like to see the world be a safer place to live."

- "I would like to empower people to be financially secure."

You develop values early in life through your contact with your environment and your subsequent experiences in it. You have developed your current value system from a variety of sources, including

- Direct instruction from teachers, clergy, and people in the community

- Your parents teaching you "right" from "wrong"

- Modeling by others in your life

- Television, movies, and books

- Values clarification processes such as the one in this chapter

THINKING ABOUT YOUR VALUES

One way to explore your values is to think about the characteristics (such as courage, honesty, athletic ability, or caring) of people you admire. These people can be living (Bill Gates) or dead (Abraham Lincoln, Mother Teresa), and they may be related to you (uncles, aunts, parents, siblings) or not (friends). Then answer the following questions:

1. What characteristics do you admire in these people?

_____

_____

2. Why do you admire these characteristics?

_____

_____

3. How can you begin to develop some of these characteristics?

_____

_____

EXPLORING YOUR VALUES

Louis Raths, an expert in the exploration of values who cowrote the pioneering book *Values and Teaching*, suggests that if you can answer yes to the following questions about a prospective value, you can be fairly certain it is a value for you:

- Do I prize this value?

- Would I defend this value publicly?

- Have I chosen this value after considering other alternatives?

- Have I thought about the consequences of expressing this value?

- Have I chosen this value freely?

- Have I acted on this value?

- Have I acted consistently and repeated a pattern of behavior regarding this value?

Your values are those internal beliefs that create standards through which your attitudes about your career and your life are formed. Whether you realize it or not, you reveal your values in how you think, what you say, and how you behave. Therefore, it is important that you learn more about your values and how they affect your choice of a major.

Learning more about your values is likely to be a lifelong process. You must be careful not to blindly follow, or choose a major, based on the values that are prescribed by society. Society's values and your values may be very different. When you are in the process of choosing a major, you need to identify what you value and then identify majors related to these values.

> **NOTE**
>
> Because we live in a diverse society, many cultural subgroups exist that have different views about money, religion, relationships, and sexual orientation. Remember that people from different cultures will also demonstrate different values. Do not assume that all people in society value the same things.

The following assessment is designed to help you explore your values as they relate to majors and occupations.

The Work Values Scale

This assessment can help you identify and explore your dominant values and how these values affect your career development. It contains 60 activity statements directly related to potential values in your life and career.

Read each of the statements and circle the number to the right that best describes how important the activity is to you according to the following scale:

> 4 = Very Important
>
> 3 = Important
>
> 2 = Somewhat Important
>
> 1 = Unimportant

This is not a test. There are no right or wrong answers, so don't spend too much time responding. Be sure to respond to every statement.

How important is it for you to...	Very Important	Important	Somewhat Important	Unimportant
1. Display good eye-hand coordination?	4	3	2	1
2. Be outdoors?	4	3	2	1
3. Be engaged in sporting events?	4	3	2	1
4. Have good motor skills?	4	3	2	1
5. Work at mechanical activities?	4	3	2	1
6. Create things with your hands?	4	3	2	1
7. Grow things outdoors?	4	3	2	1
8. Use hand tools such as hammers and screwdrivers?	4	3	2	1
9. Operate large machines and equipment?	4	3	2	1
10. Be able to repair things in your home?	4	3	2	1

Section 1 Total: _____

How important is it for you to...	Very Important	Important	Somewhat Important	Unimportant
11. Learn all you can about science?	4	3	2	1
12. Construct or interpret maps and graphs?	4	3	2	1
13. Study and test hypotheses?	4	3	2	1
14. Collect biological data?	4	3	2	1
15. Understand all you can about plants or animals?	4	3	2	1
16. Conduct scientific experiments?	4	3	2	1
17. Read about scientific or medical discoveries?	4	3	2	1
18. Read about technical developments?	4	3	2	1
19. Work with scientific knowledge and processes?	4	3	2	1
20. Solve problems by using science?	4	3	2	1

Section 2 Total: _____

How important is it for you to...	Very Important	Important	Somewhat Important	Unimportant
21. Read and/or write poetry?	4	3	2	1
22. Create beautiful things?	4	3	2	1
23. Brainstorm new ideas?	4	3	2	1
24. Design how things will work?	4	3	2	1
25. Draw or paint?	4	3	2	1
26. Develop new skills working with your hands?	4	3	2	1
27. Make music?	4	3	2	1
28. Invent new products?	4	3	2	1

	Very Important	Important	Somewhat Important	Unimportant
29. Attend theatre performances?	4	3	2	1
30. Visit museums or art galleries?	4	3	2	1

Section 3 Total: _____

How important is it for you to...

	Very Important	Important	Somewhat Important	Unimportant
31. Do volunteer work?	4	3	2	1
32. Be understanding of others' problems?	4	3	2	1
33. Give to worthwhile charities?	4	3	2	1
34. Share your money and belongings with others?	4	3	2	1
35. Do social service work?	4	3	2	1
36. Counsel other people?	4	3	2	1
37. Teach?	4	3	2	1
38. Ensure the safety and well-being of the public?	4	3	2	1
39. Be a positive role model?	4	3	2	1
40. Help people in need?	4	3	2	1

Section 4 Total: _____

How important is it for you to...

	Very Important	Important	Somewhat Important	Unimportant
41. Make important decisions?	4	3	2	1
42. Be a leader?	4	3	2	1
43. Be the boss rather than an employee?	4	3	2	1
44. Manage group projects?	4	3	2	1
45. Plan long-term goals?	4	3	2	1
46. Be considered a business expert?	4	3	2	1
47. Achieve success in business?	4	3	2	1
48. Manage the work of others?	4	3	2	1
49. Be admired by other business leaders?	4	3	2	1
50. Hold a position of authority?	4	3	2	1

Section 5 Total: _____

How important is it for you to...

	Very Important	Important	Somewhat Important	Unimportant
51. Analyze numerical data?	4	3	2	1
52. Use computers to solve problems?	4	3	2	1
53. Use statistics in your daily life?	4	3	2	1
54. Understand complex mathematical problems?	4	3	2	1
55. Use mathematical skills?	4	3	2	1
56. Be an expert at learning and remembering numbers?	4	3	2	1

(continued)

(continued)

	Very Important	Important	Somewhat Important	Unimportant
57. Calculate and compute numbers easily?	4	3	2	1
58. Manage your money effectively?	4	3	2	1
59. Follow detailed instructions?	4	3	2	1
60. Keep detailed, accurate records?	4	3	2	1

Section 6 Total: _____

Scoring

Add the numbers you have circled for each of the six sections. Put the sum in the space marked "Total" at the end of each section. Then transfer your totals for each of the sections to the following lines. Your scores in each section should range from 10 to 40.

Physical (Section 1) Total: _____

Scientific (Section 2) Total: _____

Intuitive (Section 3) Total: _____

Emotional (Section 4) Total: _____

Authoritative (Section 5) Total: _____

Logical (Section 6) Total: _____

The higher the number for each of the sections, the more important those work values are to you in making satisfying career and life choices. A high score from 31 to 40 signals a set of values that you should try to incorporate into the college major decision-making process. A score from 21 to 30 is an average score. Sections where you have a low score of 20 or less represent values that your work and career need not necessarily encompass, so they will probably not factor into your choice of a major. This isn't to suggest that those values aren't at all important to you, only that they aren't as high a priority for you. Most people will have high scores in one or two of the sections on the assessment.

Understanding the Scales

The assessment that you just completed was based on the research of Hunter Lewis. Lewis is a prominent researcher who has spent his life studying human behavior, specifically what motivates people to do the things they do. He was president of the American School of Classical Studies in Athens where he developed a system for categorizing values that are important in a person's life and career. His book, *A Question of Values: Six Ways We Make the Personal Choices That Shape Our Lives* (Axios Press, 2003), broke all values into six overarching value systems, which are described in the following sections.

Physical

People with this type of value system express a dominant interest in the use of their physical prowess, eye-hand coordination, and agility (Lewis calls this the Sensory Experience Value System).

College majors that are typically a good fit for people with this value system include the following. Check the ones that interest you:

- ☐ Anthropology
- ☐ Agriculture
- ☐ Agronomy
- ☐ Animal Sciences
- ☐ Archeology
- ☐ Broadcast Production
- ☐ Criminal Justice
- ☐ Computer-Aided Drafting

- ☐ Construction Management
- ☐ Food Science
- ☐ Forestry
- ☐ Heating and Air Conditioning
- ☐ Industrial Education
- ☐ Recreation Management
- ☐ Robotics
- ☐ Tourism

Scientific

People with this type of value system express a dominant interest in the exploration of the nature of the world or the nature of human beings. They are interested in collecting data and doing scientific research (Lewis calls this the Science Value System).

College majors that are typically a good fit for people with this value system include the following. Check the ones that interest you:

- ☐ Astronomy
- ☐ Athletic Training
- ☐ Biology
- ☐ Botany
- ☐ Biotechnology
- ☐ Chemistry
- ☐ Computer Programming
- ☐ Engineering

- ☐ Environmental Science
- ☐ Geology
- ☐ Information Systems
- ☐ Marine Biology
- ☐ Mathematics
- ☐ Nursing
- ☐ Psychology
- ☐ Zoology

Intuitive

People with this type of value system express a dominant interest in beauty, harmony, imagination, and the pursuit of art and creative expression. They are interested in turning intuition into artistic creations (Lewis called this the Intuition Value System).

College majors that are typically a good fit for people with this value system include the following. Check the ones that interest you:

☐ Advertising	☐ Graphic Design
☐ Art	☐ Interior Design
☐ Creative Writing	☐ Journalism
☐ Dance	☐ Literature
☐ English	☐ Music
☐ Fashion Design	☐ Photography
☐ Film Studies	☐ Public Relations
☐ Foreign Language	☐ Theatre

Emotional

People with this type of value system express a dominant interest in altruism and philanthropy. They are interested in helping other people and nurturing and caring for others (Lewis called this the Emotional Value System).

College majors that are typically a good fit for people with this value system include the following. Check the ones that interest you:

☐ Behavioral Science	☐ Preschool Education
☐ Child Care Management	☐ Recreation Therapy
☐ Counseling	☐ Religious Studies
☐ Early Childhood Education	☐ Secondary Education
☐ Elementary Education	☐ Social Science
☐ Human Services	☐ Social Work
☐ Middle School Education	☐ Special Education
☐ Physical Education	☐ Speech Therapy

Authoritative

People with this type of value system express a dominant interest in having power and influence and value competition and leadership as ways to achieve power (Lewis called this the Authoritative Value System).

College majors that are typically a good fit for people with this value system include the following. Check the ones that interest you:

- ☐ Banking
- ☐ Business Administration
- ☐ E-commerce
- ☐ Economics
- ☐ Entrepreneurship
- ☐ Finance
- ☐ Hotel/Motel Management
- ☐ Human Resource Management

- ☐ Industrial Relations
- ☐ Insurance
- ☐ International Business
- ☐ Management
- ☐ Marketing
- ☐ Organizational Behavior
- ☐ Pre-Law
- ☐ Restaurant Management

Logical

People with this type of value system express a dominant interest in using deductive logic, dialectics, the detection of logical fallacies, and advanced mathematical tools (Lewis called this the Logical Value System).

College majors that are typically a good fit for people with this value system include the following. Check the ones that interest you:

- ☐ Accounting
- ☐ Actuarial Science
- ☐ Banking
- ☐ Business Education
- ☐ Data Management
- ☐ Database Administrator
- ☐ City Planning
- ☐ Computer Repair

- ☐ Information Technology
- ☐ Library Science
- ☐ Materials Management
- ☐ Office Management
- ☐ Paralegal Studies
- ☐ Public Administration
- ☐ Transportation Logistics
- ☐ Urban Planning

Tying Values to Majors

What you value plays a critical role in choosing a career path. The problem is that most people have not recently thought about what they most value in life and in a career. Those who have are often the ones who are equally fortunate enough to land jobs and develop careers that mesh with their values and provide satisfying rewards. Therefore, exploring your value system is essential in choosing your college major and making other career-related decisions.

PRIORITIZING YOUR VALUES

No major at your college or university will fully incorporate all of your values. What is most important is that you choose a major that matches the values you feel strongest about. To start narrowing your choice of a major based on your values, list your three most important values, starting with the one you scored the highest in, in the spaces below. Then use the second column to list the possible majors you might be interested in that are related to that value. (Refer back to the major checklists earlier in the chapter.)

Value	Majors of Interest
_____	_____
	_____
_____	_____
	_____
_____	_____
	_____

The more you are aware of your values, the more you will understand how they affect the career decisions you make. You will begin to see a general pattern to your actions, which can then help you to plan your career. The next chapter will help you discover the role your leisure activities can play in your college major and career choices.

Consider Your Leisure Activities

People engage in a variety of leisure activities for fun everyday. For some, these activities are physical, such as golfing or bowling. Others enjoy intellectual activities, such as playing chess or solving puzzles. Still others may be creative in their spare time by writing poetry or dancing. What most people don't realize is that these activities can be clues to college majors. In this chapter, you will take a quiz to identify your leisure interests and then match them to majors that you are likely to enjoy.

The Role of Leisure in Your Career

Over the years, there has been a lack of agreement among career experts about what constitutes a career. At one time, many career counselors viewed and defined a career as the job a person had. Thus, many career counselors viewed career planning as fitting a person into the best available job. Still today, some career counselors, in describing a career, focus only on the work that their clients have done. These definitions greatly limit the clients' view of the possibilities available to them by excluding many of life's roles.

For early researchers of careers and career development, a career was the totality of work one does in a lifetime or a series of paid or unpaid occupations or jobs that a person holds throughout his or her life. Donald Super, one of the first career counselors, originally concentrated on the work one does in defining career as a continuous, lifelong process of developing and implementing a self-

concept and testing that self-concept against reality, with satisfaction to self and benefit to society. Later, he amended his definition to say that a career was the course of events that constitute a life, the sequence of occupations and other life roles that combine to express one's commitment to work in his or her total pattern of self-development.

In the late 1980s and early 1990s, many other researchers, including myself, began to view a career as something that develops over a person's life span; is unique to each person; and includes occupations and other aspects of life such as family, community, learning, and leisure. Increasingly, career counselors have helped people gain greater life satisfaction by exploring their interests in leisure-time activities.

CHARACTERISTICS OF LEISURE

Following are some of the characteristics of leisure-time activities:

- Leisure involves the use of time outside work.

- Leisure time is time free from the need to play other roles, such as those of student, parent, and citizen.

- Leisure may require effort, as in playing tennis, or it may require no effort, as in watching television.

- Leisure pursuits are often engaged in to meet some personal need, attain some value or values, and sometimes to use some ability or abilities.

- Leisure may have a clear goal, such as producing a painting, or an ill-defined goal, such as relaxing.

- Leisure activities may support, conflict with, or be neutral to one's other roles, such as that of worker, in their use of time and effort.

Leisure and Your College Major

Many of my students end up majoring in things they enjoy doing in their spare time. For example, Jennifer enjoys working out and playing tennis. She is thus considering a major in physical education.

There are several reasons why it is easy to identify a major based on leisure-time interests:

- **You have more leisure time than anything else.** I define *leisure* as any self-determined activity or experience, for which you do not receive payment, and is available to you because you have discretionary time and money. Based on this definition, anything you do, other than work, can be seen as a leisure-time activity. Therefore, the typical person spends about 8 hours a day working, 5 days a week for a total of about 40 hours per week. On the other hand, that same person has 16 hours of leisure time per day and 24 hours of leisure time every Saturday and Sunday! That totals to be 40 hours of work per week against 128 hours of leisure time. Therefore, it is often more enlightening to explore your leisure interests than interests in various jobs.

- **Leisure-time activities are more fun than work.** Let's face it, you do not engage in leisure activities that you do not like to do. But you probably have worked at jobs that you did not like. Recognize that your leisure activities can be more than simple fun; they can become your major and a job after graduation.

- **The skills you gain from leisure-time activities can easily be transferred to occupations.** People are typically good at what they enjoy, are more motivated to participate in these activities, and will spend more time at them. Therefore, people are more apt to transfer their love for leisure interests to similar majors.

Think about what you like to do in your spare time for fun and relaxation. When you have spare time, do you spend it relaxing, or playing video games with friends, or maybe even camping? Do you enjoy physical activities, such as jogging, bowling, or weight lifting? Do you enjoy creative activities, such as writing poetry, dancing, or painting pictures? Maybe you enjoy helping others by volunteering at the local hospital or tutoring others. Or do you prefer scientific leisure activities such as weather watching, amateur archeology, or astronomy? These are just a few different types of leisure activities. There are many more that you might enjoy.

DEVELOPING LEISURE ACTIVITIES

Consider what your favorite leisure activities have been at different stages of your life. What was happening in your life that steered you toward these particular leisure activities? For example, you may have started studying the stars because you had a great astronomy class in high school. List the activities and their triggers for each of the following age brackets. At this point in time, do not eliminate any activities.

Age	Activities	What Was Happening in My Life
0–10	_____	_____
	_____	_____
	_____	_____
11–20	_____	_____
	_____	_____
	_____	_____
21–30	_____	_____
	_____	_____
	_____	_____

(continued)

(continued)

Age	Activities	What Was Happening in My Life
31–40	_____	_____
	_____	_____
40+	_____	_____
	_____	_____
	_____	_____

This activity helps you explore the leisure activities that you have enjoyed over time. Consistent interest in certain types of activities is a clear indication of "true" interest. They do not have to be exact matches; simply look for patterns. For example, if you enjoyed camping when you were 10, and now you enjoy planting flowers and gardening, these show a pattern for enjoying the outdoors and nature. Now look back over the leisure activities you identified above and answer the following questions:

Which types of activities have you continued to pursue throughout your life?

_____

_____

What about these consistent activities have you enjoyed the most?

_____

_____

_____

How have your leisure interests changed over time?

_____

_____

_____

Are any of these consistent leisure interests transferable to a major and a job after graduation? If so, which majors and jobs?

_____

_____

The Leisure Activities Inventory

Leisure activities are those you do in your free time. These activities may relate to hobbies, recreation, family, volunteering, crafts, and sports. This quiz will help you identify your leisure activities. Read each statement carefully. Circle the number of the response that shows how descriptive each statement is of you. Please answer all the questions to the best of your ability using the following scale:

> 4 = Always or a Great Deal
>
> 3 = Often or Quite a Lot
>
> 2 = Sometimes or Some
>
> 1 = Rarely, if Ever

Make sure you answer every question. Remember that there are no right or wrong answers.

	Always	Often	Sometimes	Rarely
In my spare time, I enjoy...				
1. Attending art classes.	4	3	2	1
2. Drawing, painting, or sculpting.	4	3	2	1
3. Blogging, journaling, or writing poems or stories.	4	3	2	1
4. Doing crafts.	4	3	2	1
5. Singing or playing a musical instrument.	4	3	2	1
6. Attending plays or musicals.	4	3	2	1
7. Sewing and doing needlecrafts.	4	3	2	1
Section 1 Total: _____				
In my spare time, I enjoy...				
8. Hiking and camping.	4	3	2	1
9. Working on mechanical things.	4	3	2	1
10. Playing with animals.	4	3	2	1
11. Fixing things.	4	3	2	1
12. Gardening and other yard work.	4	3	2	1
13. Weight lifting or doing martial arts.	4	3	2	1
14. Playing sports.	4	3	2	1
Section 2 Total: _____				
In my spare time, I enjoy...				
15. Reading books and magazines about science.	4	3	2	1
16. Looking through a microscope.	4	3	2	1
17. Visiting museums and/or historical sites.	4	3	2	1

(continued)

(continued)

	Always	Often	Sometimes	Rarely
18. Figuring out mathematical games.	4	3	2	1
19. Looking at the stars.	4	3	2	1
20. Tracking the weather.	4	3	2	1
21. Writing computer programs.	4	3	2	1

Section 3 Total: _____

In my spare time, I enjoy...

	Always	Often	Sometimes	Rarely
22. Helping other people.	4	3	2	1
23. Volunteering.	4	3	2	1
24. Comforting friends with personal problems.	4	3	2	1
25. Teaching skills to or coaching others.	4	3	2	1
26. Playing with or entertaining children.	4	3	2	1
27. Traveling.	4	3	2	1
28. Cooking and baking.	4	3	2	1

Section 4 Total: _____

In my spare time, I enjoy...

	Always	Often	Sometimes	Rarely
29. Studying investments.	4	3	2	1
30. Leading clubs and organizations.	4	3	2	1
31. Organizing group activities.	4	3	2	1
32. Reading about the latest business trends.	4	3	2	1
33. Figuring out ways to make more money.	4	3	2	1
34. Raising funds for organizations.	4	3	2	1
35. Planning events.	4	3	2	1

Section 5 Total: _____

In my spare time, I enjoy...

	Always	Often	Sometimes	Rarely
36. Participating in "fantasy" sports leagues.	4	3	2	1
37. Developing and tracking budgets.	4	3	2	1
38. Volunteering at voting polls.	4	3	2	1
39. Repairing computers.	4	3	2	1
40. Creating web pages.	4	3	2	1
41. Controlling traffic at an event.	4	3	2	1
42. Surfing the Internet.	4	3	2	1

Section 6 Total: _____

Scoring

The inventory you just completed will help you identify various types of leisure activities that can help you choose a major. The assessment is designed to measure your leisure interests and help you identify majors related to your leisure interests. For each of the sections on the previous pages, count the scores you circled for each of the sections. Put that total on the line marked "Total" at the end of each section. Then transfer your totals to the spaces below:

> **Artistic Activities (Section 1) Total:** _____
>
> **Physical Activities (Section 2) Total:** _____
>
> **Scientific Activities (Section 3) Total:** _____
>
> **Social Activities (Section 4) Total:** _____
>
> **Authoritative Activities (Section 5) Total:** _____
>
> **Logical Activities (Section 6) Total:** _____

After you have completed transferring your total scores, find the range for your scores and use the information below to assist you in the interpretation of your scores.

If your raw score for a scale is 7 through 13, you probably are not interested in these types of leisure activities. For any scores that fall in this range, you probably do not want to consider them for a major.

If your raw score for a scale is 14 to 21, you probably have some interest in these types of leisure activities. For any scores that fall in this range, you may want to consider these areas for a potential major.

If your raw score for a scale is 22 through 28, you probably have a great deal of interest in these types of leisure activities. For any scores that fall in this range, you definitely want to consider these areas for a potential major.

Understanding the Scales

The assessment you just completed is based on a popular system for classifying occupations that was developed by John Holland. This theory suggests that you are drawn to certain leisure activities based on your personal characteristics. If your personal characteristics do not match the characteristics of a certain activity, you will not find satisfaction in it. For example, people who enjoy working with their hands may not like doing mathematical puzzles, but may enjoy fixing things that are broken. This theory suggests that people can be viewed in terms of their preferences for artistic, physical, scientific, social, authoritative, and logical activities. Read through each of the descriptions, focusing primarily on the ones in which you scored the highest.

Artistic Activities

People interested in artistic leisure activities enjoy any activity in which they can create things of beauty. They prefer to engage in imaginative activities that can be done alone. They enjoy activities where they can invent and design new products, communicate news and information, or perform for the public. People scoring high on this scale usually appreciate music and the arts.

College majors that are typically a good fit for people who enjoy artistic activities include the following. Check the ones that interest you:

- ☐ Advertising
- ☐ Art
- ☐ Creative Writing
- ☐ Dance
- ☐ English
- ☐ Fashion Design
- ☐ Film Studies
- ☐ Foreign Language
- ☐ Graphic Design
- ☐ Interior Design
- ☐ Journalism
- ☐ Literature
- ☐ Music
- ☐ Photography
- ☐ Public Relations
- ☐ Theatre

Physical Activities

People interested in physical leisure activities are primarily interested in being outdoors or using their mechanical skills. They enjoy tinkering with machines and using their hands. People scoring high on this scale are also interested in being physically active.

College majors that are typically a good fit for people who enjoy physical activities include the following. Check the ones that interest you:

- ☐ Anthropology
- ☐ Agriculture
- ☐ Agronomy
- ☐ Animal Sciences
- ☐ Archeology
- ☐ Broadcast Production
- ☐ Criminal Justice
- ☐ Computer-Aided Drafting
- ☐ Construction Management
- ☐ Food Science
- ☐ Forestry
- ☐ Heating and Air Conditioning
- ☐ Industrial Education
- ☐ Recreation Management
- ☐ Robotics
- ☐ Tourism

Scientific Activities

People interested in scientific leisure activities want to understand how things work. They value using scientific processes to discover, collect, and analyze information. They may enjoy doing research, using computers, and performing experiments.

College majors that are typically a good fit for people who enjoy scientific activities include the following. Check the ones that interest you:

☐ Astronomy	☐ Environmental Science
☐ Athletic Training	☐ Geology
☐ Biology	☐ Information Systems
☐ Botany	☐ Marine Biology
☐ Biotechnology	☐ Mathematics
☐ Chemistry	☐ Nursing
☐ Computer Programming	☐ Psychology
☐ Engineering	☐ Zoology

Social Activities

People interested in social leisure activities like to be with and help other people. They find satisfaction in making a difference in people's lives. They accomplish this in a variety of ways, from teaching and counseling to providing medical care. They generally enjoy activities that allow them to provide services to other people rather than products.

College majors that are typically a good fit for people who enjoy social activities include the following. Check the ones that interest you:

☐ Behavioral Science	☐ Preschool Education
☐ Child Care Management	☐ Recreation Therapy
☐ Counseling	☐ Religious Studies
☐ Early Childhood Education	☐ Secondary Education
☐ Elementary Education	☐ Social Science
☐ Human Services	☐ Social Work
☐ Middle School Education	☐ Special Education
☐ Physical Education	☐ Speech Therapy

Authoritative Activities

People interested in authoritative leisure activities are primarily interested in managing people or running organizations. People scoring high on this scale may enjoy positions of leadership, ensuring that people work efficiently or follow the rules. They value guiding others, solving problems, and making decisions.

College majors that are typically a good fit for people who enjoy authoritative activities include the following. Check the ones that interest you:

- ☐ Banking
- ☐ Business Administration
- ☐ E-commerce
- ☐ Economics
- ☐ Entrepreneurship
- ☐ Finance
- ☐ Hotel/Motel Management
- ☐ Human Resource Management

- ☐ Industrial Relations
- ☐ Insurance
- ☐ International Business
- ☐ Management
- ☐ Marketing
- ☐ Organizational Behavior
- ☐ Pre-Law
- ☐ Restaurant Management

Logical Activities

People interested in logical leisure activities are most interested in solving problems with deductive reasoning. They value working with numbers and having clearly defined procedures. They enjoy calculating, examining, and interpreting data and financial records.

College majors that are typically a good fit for people who enjoy logical activities include the following. Check the ones that interest you:

- ☐ Accounting
- ☐ Actuarial Science
- ☐ Banking
- ☐ Business Education
- ☐ Data Management
- ☐ Database Administrator
- ☐ City Planning
- ☐ Computer Repair

- ☐ Information Technology
- ☐ Library Science
- ☐ Materials Management
- ☐ Office Management
- ☐ Paralegal Studies
- ☐ Public Administration
- ☐ Transportation Logistics
- ☐ Urban Planning

PUTTING YOUR LEISURE ACTIVITIES AND COLLEGE MAJOR TOGETHER

To use your leisure activities as a guide to a college major that you would enjoy, list your favorite types of leisure activities, starting with the scale you scored the highest in on the Leisure Activities Inventory. Then, using your results from the majors checklists, list the majors that relate to your leisure interests and appeal to you.

Your highest scoring leisure activity scale:

_____

Matching majors of interest within that scale:

_____

_____

Your second highest scoring leisure activity scale:

_____

Matching majors of interest within that scale:

_____

_____

Your third highest scoring leisure activity scale:

_____

Matching majors of interest within that scale:

_____

_____

Remember that leisure is much more than those things you do other than work. Leisure is an important part of your career development and can be indicative of those things you like and have liked over the course of your life. You engage in leisure-time activities because they are fun and provide you with a certain amount of satisfaction, or you would stop doing them. When you are trying to choose a major, pay particular attention to your developmental leisure interests. They may easily transfer or at least relate to a major and a job after graduation. As Confucius said, "Find a job you love, and you will never have to work a day in your life." The next chapter will help you to begin doing research and gathering information about majors and occupations of interest.

PART 4: DEVELOP AN ACTION PLAN

"It isn't sufficient just to want——you've got to ask yourself what you are going to do to get the things you want."

—Franklin D. Roosevelt

Research, Research, Research

Now that you have a strong sense of your skills, interests, values, and personality, it is time to put this information to work by translating it into career information that you can use to make an effective decision about majors. Your goal is to gather as much information about potential occupations (and potential majors) as you possibly can. This chapter will explore some of the tools people use to research career and occupational options. This exploration process will help you to focus your efforts and begin to narrow the search for the best major for you. The quiz in this chapter, the Majors Research Scale, will help you determine how close you are to choosing a college major.

Career Maturity and College

My wife, Kathy, knew that she wanted to be an elementary teacher since she was a little girl. When she was young, she used to set her younger brother down and conduct classes on such topics as types of dogs and how to play baseball, whether he wanted to learn about them or not.

As a teenager, Kathy worked at the local swimming pool, where she taught people how to swim and dive. She also worked in her church watching the younger children and teaching Bible School lessons. When she enrolled in college, she knew what she wanted to major in and what career path she wanted to follow. Just to make sure, though, she took an education course her first semester.

On the other hand, I started college with no idea what I wanted to major in. I had a lot of diverse interests: reading and writing; learning about social sciences such as history, sociology, and psychology; participating in outdoor activities; and learning languages. Criminal justice (the occupation of many of my favorite television characters) appealed to me. I also thought about working with people who stuttered. How could I possibly settle on one thing to major in and do as an occupation for the rest of my life? I kept telling everybody that I surely would get a sign pointing me in the direction of a great major if I were patient enough. No sign came, though.

Although these two examples are the extremes, they demonstrate the variation in career maturity that students bring to a college or university in their freshman year. *Career maturity* is a fancy name for how knowledgeable you are about what you might like to pursue while you are attending college. Career development expert Donald Super described the term *career maturity* as your progress in relation to your career tasks and goals. It refers to your ability to make informed career decisions based on knowledge about yourself and research related to the world of work. Therefore, the more you have learned about yourself from completing the quizzes in this book, and the more research you conduct based on the information in this chapter, the more career mature you would be considered.

You are probably somewhere in between the two extremes you just read about. You may have some ideas and may have even narrowed your decision to several options. However, if you do not know what your potential major is, know that you are not alone. Most colleges and universities have a great many students who begin their college careers as "undecided" majors. There is no shame in being an undecided major student. Undecided is a great place to be until you can choose a major that fits you like a glove. College is a perfect place for you to begin exploring your different values, interests, and skills, and this book can help you focus your efforts in this exploration process.

While taking different classes and exploring different majors, you may simply confirm talents and interests that you already knew you possessed. On the other hand, you may discover talents and strengths that you never realized you had. For example, James took a sociology class his first semester and learned that he did not like to analyze numbers and data or present information in front of a class, but he did like to study people and patterns of behavior. From this one class, James was able to learn about his likes and dislikes, as well as information about his skills and introverted personality type. Therefore, it is important to remember that although all of your explorations may not match your personal characteristics, all of your experiences will help you to clarify who you truly are and what you want to do with the rest of your life.

The College Majors Research Scale

To identify the best major for you, you need to do a lot of research about majors. There are a variety of ways that you can accomplish this research. The Majors Research Scale is designed to help you explore how much time you have put into conducting research about the various majors offered at your college or university.

The following quiz consists of 20 items that help you explore how proactive you have been in gathering information for your choice of a major. Respond to each item using the following scale:

> 3 = A Lot
>
> 2 = A Little
>
> 1 = Not at All

	A Lot	A Little	Not at All
How much time have you spent researching majors?			
1. I have talked to professors and staff in various departments.	3	2	1
2. I have talked to other students in a variety of majors.	3	2	1
3. I know which majors are in demand to employers.	3	2	1
4. I have explored potential minors.	3	2	1
5. I have explored the course offerings in various majors.	3	2	1
6. I can describe majors of interest in concrete and specific terms.	3	2	1
7. I have learned about occupations related to majors that interest me.	3	2	1
8. I know what majors are offered at the college.	3	2	1
9. I have read descriptions of majors in the college catalog.	3	2	1
10. I have talked with a professional counselor about my options.	3	2	1
11. I have volunteered for different organizations in order to learn more about occupations.	3	2	1
12. I have a specific major in mind.	3	2	1
13. I have talked with my parents about majors.	3	2	1
14. I have talked to people working in a variety of occupations about majors.	3	2	1
15. I have looked in textbooks for information about majors.	3	2	1
16. I don't let others' expectations influence my thoughts about majors.	3	2	1
17. I have explored information about majors on the Internet.	3	2	1
18. I have researched information about majors on the Internet.	3	2	1
19. I know how to declare a major.	3	2	1
20. I enjoy researching majors of interest.	3	2	1
Total: _____			

Scoring

The Majors Research Scale provides you with information about how much time you have spent so far gathering research about potential majors available to you. Add the numbers you have circled above. Put that total on the line marked "Total" at the end of the quiz.

A low score from 20 to 33 indicates that you have not spent much time researching and exploring various majors offered at your college or university. A moderate score from 34 to 46 indicates that you have spent some time researching and exploring various majors offered at your college or university. A high score from 47 to 60 indicates that you have spent a great deal of time researching and exploring various majors offered at your college or university. If your score is low, the information in the rest this chapter will help you dive into the process of exploring majors and related occupations. If your score is moderate or even high, you may discover a tool in this information that you haven't yet tried, which may help you refine your ideas about what you want your major to be.

Information About Majors

You can start your research on college majors the way you would start researching any other topic: at the library and on the Internet. College course catalogs also provide a wealth of information.

REVIEWING BOOKS FOR COLLEGE MAJOR INFORMATION

Make a list of three majors you are currently thinking about exploring. List them below and then go to the bookstore and the library and look at books that relate to that major. Then list what you liked and disliked about each major subject after reading about it.

Major	What I Liked	What I Disliked

What patterns do you notice when you look at your responses?

_____

_____

_____

Online Research

A great source of information about occupations and majors is the Internet. You might want to search Internet sources for information about majors of interest to you. There are many popular websites specifically designed to provide you with information about majors and occupations that are related to various majors:

The College Board: www.collegeboard.com/csearch/majors_careers/profiles/

College Majors 101: http://collegemajors101.com

MyMajors.com: www.mymajors.com/list-of-majors-in-college.cfml

Princeton Review: www.princetonreview.com/majors.aspx

College Course Catalogs

When you are considering different options for your college major, you need to spend some time learning about the courses and requirements of the different fields of study. It can be difficult to tell what is involved in a particular major based simply on its name. For example, it would probably be difficult for you to tell the difference between a marketing major and an advertising major, although differences do exist.

College course catalogs can be an excellent resource for helping you find college major descriptions and a list of required courses. Most schools publish their catalogs online for easy access. This way you can explore the college catalogs of various schools with programs of interest to you.

QUESTIONS FOR ANALYZING A MAJOR

When you are researching college major information, ask yourself the following:

- What types of specialized skills will I need to study this major?
- What courses will I need to graduate with this major?
- How difficult would the coursework in this field be for me?
- Where do people graduating with this major work after graduation?

Occupational Information

Gathering specific occupational information about work environments and industries in which you might like to work is important. This research process will be full of surprises, so keep an open mind. The more you gather occupational information, the more you might discover occupations that interest you. That is the power of the exploration process.

For example, Sally always thought that she wanted to be a nurse. However, after researching various occupational titles and gathering occupational information, she learned about an occupation titled medical technologist that was closely related to nursing but was a better fit for her personal characteristics.

As you begin this process, go back and review your results from the previous chapters so that the occupations you explore will match your interests, skills, values, and personality. After you have completed this process, you will have identified several job titles about which you would like to make decisions.

You can learn a lot about occupations by simply reading books and career pamphlets. These resources provide information that you can use to determine whether an occupation is suited to your personal characteristics. Most job descriptions will include a list of job duties, working conditions, average earnings, the training and education required, and the outlook for that particular occupation. You can compare all of this data to the information you gathered about yourself in the first two parts of this book to find a major that matches your interests, values, skills, and needs.

Use the following sources of occupational information to gather information about specific occupations of interest to you. An exploration worksheet is included after the list to help you gather the information you need.

- *Occupational Outlook Handbook (OOH):* The *OOH* is developed by the United States Department of Labor and presents occupations by career families. For each occupation, the *OOH* provides information about job duties, working conditions, level and places of employment, education and training requirements, job employment outlook, advancement possibilities, earnings, and related occupations. You can find it in most libraries or online at www.bls.gov/oco/.

- **Occupational Information Network (O*NET):** The O*NET is a computerized database of information about occupations. O*NET provides information on nearly 1,000 occupations, including descriptions of the occupation, occupational task list, earnings and education, general work activities, and correlations with other career resources. It is available at libraries or online at www.onetonline.org.

- *New Guide for Occupational Exploration (GOE):* This book allows you to explore all major O*NET jobs based on your interests. It also corresponds directly to the 16 career clusters used in Chapter 4. Thus you can use your knowledge of your interests and skills to search directly for even more jobs that would be a good fit.

EXPLORING OCCUPATIONAL INFORMATION

Complete this worksheet for each potential occupation you research.

Title of occupation: _____

Description of the occupation:

_____

_____

_____

Nature of the work and job functions performed:

_____

_____

_____

Education and training needed:

_____

_____

Skills and abilities needed:

_____

_____

Salary range: _____

Working conditions:

_____

_____

Employment outlook:

_____

_____

Related occupations:

_____

_____

IDENTIFYING OCCUPATIONS RELATED TO MAJORS

In the following table, identify some of the majors that are of interest to you and then list some of the occupational titles that accompany those majors.

Majors of Interest   **Some Occupational Titles**

_____   _____

                                 _____

                                 _____

_____   _____

                                 _____

                                 _____

_____   _____

                                 _____

                                 _____

CRITICAL THINKING QUESTIONS

As you research majors and occupations, think about your answers to these questions based on the information you have discovered, including what you have learned about yourself in previous chapters.

- What does this information mean to me?
- In what ways is the information accurate?
- In what ways is the information less than accurate?
- How do I feel about the information?
- What surprised me most about my research?
- How is this information different from what I already know?
- What types of majors does this information lead to?

Informational Interviews

A good place to start researching majors and occupations is by talking to people you know and asking for suggestions and advice about the best fit of a major for you. These should be people who know you and know about various majors on a college campus.

ASKING PEOPLE YOU KNOW FOR COLLEGE MAJOR ADVICE

Ask three or four friends, family members, or other students for their advice about the best college major options for you. List the people you have contacted below and what they suggested to you.

People I Contacted	Their Suggestions About Majors
_____	_____
	_____
	_____
_____	_____
	_____
	_____
_____	_____
	_____

What patterns do you notice when you look at the information provided?

_____

_____

_____

_____

To get a clearer picture about majors and occupations, you may also want to conduct some informational interviews to learn about various majors and the occupations tied to those majors. You probably will have to go beyond your immediate circle of family and friends to connect with students in your classes, professors, administrators, and people who are working in the fields you are interested in.

WHAT TO SAY TO SET UP AN INFORMATIONAL INTERVIEW

When you are asking other people for information about occupations and college majors, you may want to rehearse what to say to gather the information. You should probably prepare a short introduction to yourself and what type of information you are seeking.

For example, you could approach a fellow student by saying the following:

"Hello, my name is Rachel. I am a freshman and undecided about a major. I noticed that you are majoring in advertising. After class, could we meet up and talk for a few minutes about what it is like to be an advertising major?"

If you want to speak to an academic advisor, you might use the following script:

"Hello, my name is Michael, and I am a freshman. I am undecided about my major, but I might want to be an art major. As the academic advisor for the College of Fine Arts, you are knowledgeable about the various majors housed in it. Could I talk with you for about 15 minutes to review some of the requirements of an art degree and some of the job opportunities that might be available upon graduation?"

Current Students

A good way to get a realistic picture of what a certain college major is like is to talk with students who are already enrolled in degree programs in that major. Following are some of the questions you may want to ask:

- Why did you choose this major?
- What types of classes have you completed?
- What do you like about the major?
- What do you dislike about the major?
- What types of jobs are you interested in when you graduate?

TALKING WITH OTHER STUDENTS ABOUT COLLEGE MAJORS

Find at least three junior or senior students who have majors that interest you and interview them. Then fill out the blanks below.

Name of student: _____

Major: _____

What new, surprising, or persuasive opinions or information did this person share?

_____

_____

_____

Name of student: _____

Major: _____

What new, surprising, or persuasive opinions or information did this person share?

_____

_____

_____

Name of student: _____

Major: _____

What new, surprising, or persuasive opinions or information did this person share?

_____

_____

_____

Professors and Administrators

Another place to learn about majors on campus is by contacting professors in various academic departments, college admissions officers, academic advisors, and career services center staff. Following are some questions you may want to ask:

- What is unique about this major program?

- What are the primary skills needed to succeed in this major?

- What occupations do most students in this major go into after graduation?

- How much demand will there be for people graduating with this major?

- What is the starting pay for someone graduating in this major?

- Do most graduates with this major go to graduate school or directly into the world of work?

INTERVIEWING CAMPUS PROFESSIONALS

Ask three or four student personnel professionals at your college or university to help you in the majors exploration process with advice about majors that might link to your interests, skills, personality, and values. List the people you have contacted below and what they suggested to you.

People I Contacted   **Their Suggestions About Majors**

_____   _____

                                   _____

                                   _____

_____   _____

                                   _____

_____   _____

                                   _____

What patterns do you notice when you look at the information provided?

_____

_____

_____

_____

Working Professionals

Another place to learn about majors on campus is by contacting people who are successfully employed in fields of interest to you. In an informational interview, you can gather information about the person's job duties, working conditions, and much more.

Interviewing people for information about occupations does not have to be as difficult as it sounds. Informational interviews can be a formal scheduled meeting or an informal, quick conversation in the parking lot. You can begin this process with people you know such as friends, relatives, and neighbors.

Here are some tips for gathering occupational information from professionals working in specific occupations of interest to you:

- Be assertive and ask people for their help. Most people will be gracious and provide you with the information you need.

- Remember that the Career Services Center at your college or university might have a list of alumni who can provide you with information about occupations and maybe even act as mentors to you while you are in the major selection process.

- Focus on conducting occupational interviews with people in occupations of interest to you. These interviews will help you begin expanding or narrowing your options.

- Keep reviewing the results of the assessments you have completed in this book as you gather information in your informational interviews. These results might provide you with a guideline to choosing the best professionals to interview.

- Use social networking sites, such as Facebook and LinkedIn, to gather occupational information quickly and efficiently.

- Write down the information you learn from the interviews so you can refer to it later. You can use the Exploring Occupational Information worksheet provided in this chapter for this purpose or the following worksheet.

Following are some questions you may want to ask:

- What characteristics do the people in your occupation have in common?

- What did the majority of the people whom you know with this job major in?

- How did you prepare for your career?

- What did you major in?

- What was it like to major in that?

- What did you like most about your college major?

- If you had to go through college again, what would you do differently?

- What is the future of your occupation?

LEARNING FROM PROFESSIONALS ABOUT OCCUPATIONS AND MAJORS

Ask three working professionals if you could spend some time with them to learn a little bit about what type of work they do. (Refer to the box titled "What to Say to Set Up an Informational Interview" for ideas on how to do this.) During the interview, ask for career advice or advice about majors that might link to your interests, skills, personality, and values. List the names of the people you contacted and what they suggested to you below.

Name of professional: _____

Occupation: _____

What new, surprising, or persuasive opinions or information did this person share?

_____

_____

_____

Name of professional: _____

Occupation: _____

What new, surprising, or persuasive opinions or information did this person share?

_____

_____

_____

Name of professional: _____

Occupation: _____

What new, surprising, or persuasive opinions or information did this person share?

_____

_____

_____

This chapter has presented many different ways for you to gather additional information about the majors offered at your college or university. Some of the methods described in this chapter may be easier for you to complete than others. The secret is to use as many of them as you possibly can so that you can make a more informed decision about your major. The next chapter will assist you with the decision-making process.

Try Different Decision-Making Styles

The ability to make effective decisions determines how satisfied we are in many aspects of our lives. We make decisions every day, from what clothes to wear to what food to eat. Although there are many different approaches to making decisions, we tend to favor a single approach that is largely based on our personality.

Of course, some decisions are bigger than simply choosing clothing and food. The choice of a major, for example, is a big decision that can impact the rest of your career. Look back at some of the big decisions you have made in the past. How did you make these decisions? In this chapter, you take a quiz to assess your primary decision-making style. Then you explore how to use this style in combination with different decision-making styles to choose a college major.

The Decision-Making Style Scale

The Decision-Making Style Scale is designed to help you understand how you currently make decisions in life and to give you additional skills. This scale contains statements that are divided into four categories. Read each of the statements and decide how descriptive the statement is of you. Circle the number of your response on the line to the right of each statement, using the following scale.

4 = A Lot Like Me

3 = Somewhat Like Me

2 = A Little Like Me

1 = Not Like Me

This is not a test, and there are no right or wrong answers. Do not spend too much time thinking about your answers. Your initial response will likely be the most true for you. Be sure to respond to every statement.

	A Lot Like Me	Somewhat Like Me	A Little Like Me	Not Like Me
When I make decisions,...				
1. I look at them logically.	4	3	2	1
2. I analyze the facts and put them in order.	4	3	2	1
3. I want to find the one right answer.	4	3	2	1
4. I analyze the situation objectively.	4	3	2	1
5. I pay attention to all details of the problem.	4	3	2	1
6. I hesitate to add emotions to the decision situation.	4	3	2	1
7. I concentrate on the decision and nothing else.	4	3	2	1
Section 1 Total: _____				
When I make decisions,...				
8. I try to make decisions based on intuitive, "gut" feelings.	4	3	2	1
9. I look at the big picture, not small details.	4	3	2	1
10. I do what feels right.	4	3	2	1
11. I always look for new, creative ways to make them.	4	3	2	1
12. I rely on internal signals about what feels good.	4	3	2	1
13. I focus on the meaning of the decision to all involved.	4	3	2	1
14. I value insights over facts.	4	3	2	1
Section 2 Total: _____				
When I make decisions,...				
15. I focus on what is happening around me.	4	3	2	1
16. I pay attention to specifics and details.	4	3	2	1
17. I look for the immediate costs and benefits.	4	3	2	1
18. I look for a practical solution to the problem.	4	3	2	1
19. I look at the decision realistically.	4	3	2	1

	A Lot Like Me	Somewhat Like Me	A Little Like Me	Not Like Me
20. I rely on experience and standard ways to help me decide.	4	3	2	1
21. I gather as many facts as possible.	4	3	2	1
		Section 3 Total: _____		
When I make decisions,...				
22. My values play a large part.	4	3	2	1
23. I think about the people involved as much as the task.	4	3	2	1
24. I try to sense how others feel about my decisions.	4	3	2	1
25. I want the best solution for everyone involved.	4	3	2	
26. I use my emotions as part of the process.	4	3	2	1
27. I follow my heart.	4	3	2	1
28. I do not analyze the problem in a logical way.	4	3	2	1
		Section 4 Total: _____		

Scoring

The Decision-Making Style Scale is designed to measure your approach to making choices and solving problems that occur in your life, relationships, and career. For each of the four sections, add the numbers you circled for each of the statements. Put that total on the line marked "Total" at the end of each section.

Then transfer your totals to the spaces below:

> **Thinking (Section 1) Total:** _____
>
> **Intuitive (Section 2) Total:** _____
>
> **Sensing (Section 3) Total:** _____
>
> **Feeling (Section 4) Total:** _____

The area in which you scored the highest tends to be your preferred decision-making style. Similarly, the area in which you scored the lowest tends to be your least-used style for making important decisions.

Understanding the Scales

The Decision-Making Style Scale is loosely based on several of the dimensions measured by the Myers-Briggs Type Indicator (MBTI), a widely used personality and career assessment. The MBTI is based on psychiatrist Carl Jung's ideas about perception, judgment, and attitudes in human personality. However, these dimensions also play an important role in how you go about making

decisions in your life. The following descriptions are provided to help you in better understanding how you will ultimately make your college major decision. You should read through each of the descriptions to better understand how different people make their decisions, but you need to focus on the scale in which you scored highest. That is your preferred decision-making style.

Thinking

A Thinking decision-making style involves the exploration of the problem and the effects of your environment. In this approach, you identify the decision that has to be made, explore alternatives before making a final decision, and develop a plan for making an effective decision based on information. You carefully weigh the costs and benefits of the various decisions. You gather and consider additional information about alternatives and the possible consequences of each alternative. The ultimate decision you make is based on a logical problem-solving approach.

If this is your style, the following statements are most likely true:

- You are analytical.
- You use cause-and-effect reasoning.
- You rely on logic.
- You are reasonable.
- You have good common sense.
- You want everyone to be treated the same.
- You are energized by critiquing possible alternatives.
- You like to mentally remove yourself from the situation.

EVALUATING THE THINKING DECISION-MAKING STYLE

Describe a time when the Thinking decision-making style has worked well for you.

_____

_____

_____

_____

Describe a time when the Thinking decision-making style has not worked well for you.

_____

_____

_____

_____

Intuitive

An Intuitive decision-making style is one in which you make decisions based on "gut-level" reactions. You tend to rely on your internal signals and identify and choose an alternative based on what you feel is the best. You do not spend a lot of time collecting facts and gathering information before you make a decision. You often make important decisions based on hunches or your "sixth sense" about the decision to be made.

> **NOTE**
>
> The Intuitive style can be useful when limited factual data is available. However, do not simply substitute intuition for the information gathering you need to do to make a decision.

If this is your style, the following statements are most likely true:

- You are oriented to the future.

- You communicate creatively.

- You develop imaginative alternatives.

- You move quickly to solutions, based on your hunches.

- You look for similarities in other decisions you have needed to make.

- You need the potential decision to make sense to you.

- You are attuned to seeing new possibilities.

- You see the big picture.

EVALUATING THE INTUITIVE DECISION-MAKING STYLE

Describe a time when the Intuitive decision-making style has worked well for you.

_____

_____

_____

_____

Describe a time when the Intuitive decision-making style has not worked well for you.

_____

_____

_____

_____

Sensing

A Sensing decision-making style is one in which you take in information that is real and tangible. You want to know what really is happening with the decision you are about to make. You are observant about the specifics of what is going on around you and are especially attuned to the practical realities of the situation. You tend to notice specifics and enjoy looking at the facts. You may overlook recurring themes, focusing instead on the factual and the concrete issues involved in choosing a major. You will rely on and trust your previous experience in dealing with similar decisions.

If this is your style, the following statements are most likely true:

- You are oriented to the present.

- You focus on the real and actual.

- You trust your experience from previous decision situations.

- You trust facts rather than other people.

- You are observant.

- You are able to remember specifics about the decision.

- You understand ideas through practical applications.

- You build carefully toward conclusions.

EVALUATING THE SENSING DECISION-MAKING STYLE

Describe a time when the Sensing decision-making style has worked well for you.

_____

_____

_____

_____

Describe a time when the Sensing decision-making style has not worked well for you.

_____

_____

_____

_____

Feeling

A Feeling decision-making style is one in which you want to find the best answer based on your feelings, tending primarily to rely on your emotions and values. With this style, you are most comfortable when you add emotion to the decision to be made. You will most often depend on a subjective analysis of the problem, rather than focusing on facts and figures. You try to mentally place yourself in the other person's or people's places so that you can identify with them. You will make decisions based on your value system.

If this is your style, the following statements are most likely true:

- You are empathetic to others in the situation.
- You are guided by your own personal issues.
- You are compassionate.
- You assess the impact of the decision on other people.
- You strive for harmony in resolving problems.
- Others call you tenderhearted.
- You always try to treat others fairly.
- You believe that positive interactions are critical in decision making.

EVALUATING THE FEELING DECISION-MAKING STYLE

Describe a time when the Feeling decision-making style has worked well for you.

_____

_____

_____

_____

Describe a time when the Feeling decision-making style has not worked well for you.

_____

_____

_____

_____

The Decision-Making Process

There is no simple step-by-step process that guarantees you a perfect decision to every question in your life. The decision-making process is a search for, and implementation of, the best possible alternative(s). As a decision maker, you will develop your own method for making big decisions, like the one you face in choosing a college major. One of the best methods for doing this is to try using the most effective aspects of the four different styles. The following worksheet is a guide in how you can integrate the four styles in the decision-making process.

INTEGRATING MULTIPLE DECISION-MAKING STYLES

Step 1: Define the decision. Use the Sensing style to see the decision as it really is. Start by examining the results of the quizzes you have completed in this book.

For the quizzes in Part 2, look back to Chapters 4, 5, and 6 and place a check mark by the clusters that represent your top five scores in each area. Thus, you would look back to the Career Interests Inventory you took, identify the top five clusters, and go down the column below, placing a check mark next to each of the five clusters in the Interests column. Then do the same for skills and courses.

Cluster	Interests	Skills	Courses	Total
Cluster 1				
Cluster 2				
Cluster 3				
Cluster 4				
Cluster 5				
Cluster 6				
Cluster 7				
Cluster 8				
Cluster 9				
Cluster 10				
Cluster 11				
Cluster 12				
Cluster 13				
Cluster 14				
Cluster 15				
Cluster 16				

Add the number of check marks in each row and write the number in the Total column. To determine which cluster of majors fits you best, write the cluster with the highest total here: _____.

For the quizzes in Part 3, refer back to Chapters 7, 8, and 9. List the top six majors of interest that matched your personality, values, and leisure activities. Circle any majors that appear in more than one list:

Personality	**Values**	**Leisure Activities**
_____	_____	_____
_____	_____	_____
_____	_____	_____
_____	_____	_____
_____	_____	_____
_____	_____	_____

Step 2: Consider the possibilities. Use the Intuitive style to brainstorm all your possible college major alternatives.

What other ways can you look at the problem? Consider double majors, minors, and other programs that your college offers that would be the best fit for you.

_____

_____

What does the information that you have gathered suggest to you?

_____

_____

How does your major connect to the career you want?

_____

_____

Review your answers in Step 1. Go to the appendix and read the descriptions of majors in the cluster you listed. Also look at the majors you circled. Consider these options, and then list three possible majors below. (If you are already enrolled in college, make sure these majors are offered at your school!)

Major 1: _____

Major 2: _____

Major 3: _____

(continued)

(continued)

Step 3: Consider the consequences. To make the decision using the Thinking style, consider the outcomes of the different majors you can choose:

What are the pros of each option?

Major 1: _____

Major 2: _____

Major 3: _____

What are the cons of each option?

Major 1: _____

Major 2: _____

Major 3: _____

What are the logical consequences of each option?

Major 1: _____

Major 2: _____

Major 3: _____

Step 4: Weigh the alternatives. Use the Feeling style to evaluate each possible major. You can do so by answering some of the following questions:

How does each alternative fit with my values?

Major 1: _____

Major 2: _____

Major 3: _____

Is there any new information you have obtained that may affect your decision about any major?

Major 1: _____

Major 2: _____

Major 3: _____

Are there any risks involved with any of the choices? For example, your parents may not approve of one of your options, thus you risk making them angry.

Major 1: _____

Major 2: _____

Major 3: _____

How will each alternative enhance positive interactions?

Major 1: _____

Major 2: _____

Major 3: _____

Step 5: Make a final decision. Complete the following sentence:

I have decided to major in _____.

What have you decided about a dual major or a minor?

_____

Step 6: Act on your decision. Complete the following sentence:

I will implement my college major decision by

_____

_____

_____

The purpose of this chapter was to teach a decision-making model that you can use for future career decisions. If you used this model, you should have made a decision and chosen a college major. Remember that you create the type of career you desire by the quality of the decisions you make. By making good decisions, you can move closer to your career dreams. In addition, being able to make decisions that lead to growth will help you live a healthier and less stressful life. The next chapter will help you explore how you are motivated to achieve your career goals and dreams.

Find Your Goal Motivation

Goals are often equated with success, ambition, hopes, and dreams. You hear talk about goals in a variety of settings. For example, you have probably heard a football coach say that his goal is to win the championship next year or a sales manager say that her goal for next year is a million dollars' worth of sales. Goals tend to be the end result, and that end result is usually some success or achievement. As you are reading this book, one of your goals is to choose a college major that will bring you internal and external rewards.

Knowing why goals matter to you is important. How will choosing a major make a positive change in your life? What will it take for you to achieve the goal of choosing and implementing the major that will bring you both internal and external rewards? What will you need to do to achieve success in choosing a major? How is your choice going to affect your life and career? These are important questions for you to think about.

Everyone commits to his or her goals for specific reasons. The purpose of this chapter is to help you explore what is motivating you in making the choice of a college major. The more the major you choose ties into your goal motivation system, the greater the effort you will put into it through graduation.

Internal and External Motivators

Motivation is one of the most powerful forces that propel you to achieve your goals. There are two basic types of motivation: internal and external. Internal motivation comes from within and is

largely determined by your values and the goals you set. It is the drive to do things that are interesting, challenging, and rewarding to you. This type of motivation is powerful and easier to maintain because it suggests that you are doing something because you enjoy it. If you were pursuing a college degree based solely on internal motivators, you would do so even if there were no tangible results when you were finished, and you would take courses for the joy of learning.

In a perfect world, gaining knowledge would be the reason that most people pursued a college degree. However, this view is a little unrealistic. External motivation usually plays a part in the decision to go to college. This type of motivation comes from sources outside you. It is the desire to do something because you know it will bring you rewards, such as increased income, benefits, or praise from others.

People who pursue goals based on external motivation engage in activities, not because they enjoy them, but because they want the external reward that is the end result of the activities. People who are externally motivated will pursue a task as long they believe the external motivator to be present. An example would be a person who dislikes learning but goes to college to earn a degree in order to get a marketing job when she graduates.

Of course, being successful in college requires a certain amount of internal and external motivation. People attending college because they want to learn new things and further their education will likely feel the pull to be successful simply because of the nature of college. They will exhibit high levels of motivation, effort, and persistence in pursuing their degrees. However, most people would not choose to pursue further education without a payoff in the end. Thus, people who are motivated both internally and externally will be the most successful in attaining a college degree.

It is logical to surmise that everyone who goes to college does so because he or she has a course of study he or she would like to pursue and turn into a career. However, the opposite is often true. You might be one of the people who know you need to be in college to excel in your career, but do not know the path that will lead to success. If so, relax; you are not alone.

Let's take a look at two students with whom I have recently worked. Jim is not sure what he wants to do with his life, but he is sure that he wants to make a lot of money. He is more interested in what he will receive after completing college, such as a high-paying job and financial security. He is interested in the changes that have occurred in society and the world of work and how those changes will dictate the types of jobs that will be in demand in the future. He is confident that once he identifies some good-paying occupations, he will be able to find the best major to fit him and his characteristics. He wants to keep his eye on the prize though—financial security.

For Jim, college (and the choice of a college major) is tied to external rewards. His external motivator is money and material things, and that's okay. All people want to live comfortably and find financial security through the work they do.

However, there is more to work than the money you will make over a lifetime. All of the money in the world is not enough if you hate your job and don't feel a sense of purpose in what you are doing. Therefore, internal satisfaction also plays some role in your college major choice.

Sheri also is not sure what she wants to do with her life, but she is sure that she wants to find an occupation (and a major) that is related to her interests, personality, and values. She is motivated internally to reach her full potential while also helping to make the world a better place to live. She is interested in occupations that make a difference in the lives of other people. She loves to learn and wants to use her knowledge to help other people thrive. She is not worried about how much a job pays, just that she is happy. For Sheri, college (and the choice of a college major) is tied to internal rewards such as reaching her full potential, lifelong learning, and helping other people.

Although these two examples are at the extreme ends of the motivation continuum, they provide excellent examples of how internal and external motivators can influence your choice of a major. One way of getting the best of both worlds is to harness the power of both internal and external motivation. To do this, choose a major that leads to occupations that match your interests, skills, and personality (internal motivation). But don't forget to also take into account job availability, job growth, and salary (external motivation). Choosing a major that incorporates both internal and external motivation is the surest way to earning a college degree and finding occupational satisfaction.

The Educational Motivation Scale

The Educational Motivation Scale is designed to help you identify how important external and internal motivation is in your choice of a college major. Please read each statement carefully. Then using the following scale, circle the number that best describes how important each item is in your choice of a college major:

> 3 = Very Important
>
> 2 = Somewhat Important
>
> 1 = Not Important

Keep in mind that there are no right or wrong answers. Please circle only one number for each item.

	Very Important	Somewhat Important	Not Important
I want a major that will…			
1. Allow me to learn all I can.	3	2	1
2. Focus my attention on things outside myself.	3	2	1
3. Be fun to learn about.	3	2	1
4. Improve my life.	3	2	1
5. Gratify me.	3	2	1
6. Teach me to think critically and creatively.	3	2	1
7. Easily fit into my identity.	3	2	1

(continued)

(continued)

	Very Important	Somewhat Important	Not Important
8. Interest me, regardless of its income potential.	3	2	1
9. Help me to achieve my full potential.	3	2	1
10. Allow me to make a valuable contribution to society.	3	2	1
11. Develop my talents.	3	2	1
12. Help me feel good about myself.	3	2	1
13. Put me in charge of my own destiny.	3	2	1
14. Promote personal growth.	3	2	1
15. Fascinate me to the point that I forget about everything else.	3	2	1

Section 1 Total: _____

I want a major that will...

	Very Important	Somewhat Important	Not Important
16. Enable me to make lots of money.	3	2	1
17. Lead to a job with good benefits.	3	2	1
18. Train me for a job that will still be in demand in the future.	3	2	1
19. Increase my income potential.	3	2	1
20. Improve my professional skills.	3	2	1
21. Boost the amount of recognition and praise I receive.	3	2	1
22. Make me more employable.	3	2	1
23. Give me skills that are transferable from job to job.	3	2	1
24. Prepare me for a job with job security.	3	2	1
25. Help me earn enough to provide for me and my family.	3	2	1
26. Enhance the lifestyle I can afford.	3	2	1
27. Give me more professional options.	3	2	1
28. Advance my career.	3	2	1
29. Protect me from being unemployed.	3	2	1
30. Enable me to buy nice things.	3	2	1

Section 2 Total: _____

Scoring

Add up the scores you circled for the two sections of the assessment. Put each total on the line marked "Total" at the end of the section. For each section, you will get a total ranging from 15 to 45. Then transfer your totals to the spaces below:

Internal Motivation (Section 1): _____

External Motivation (Section 2): _____

Scores from 36 to 45 on the individual scales are high and indicate that you possess a great deal of that particular type of motivation. Scores from 26 to 35 on the individual scales are average and indicate that you possess some of that particular type of motivation. Scores from 15 to 25 on the individual scales are low and indicate that you do not possess much of that particular type of motivation.

Understanding the Scales

Internal motivation is your willingness to act based on the potential satisfaction you will receive from the experience of attending college. External motivation is your willingness to act based on the potential rewards you will receive from the experience of attending college. To get the most out of your college major and overall college experience, you should aim to strike a balance between the two. If you scored low in either type of motivation, pay particular attention to the questions in the following related worksheets. You may need to rethink your decision in order to choose a major for which you can sustain the necessary motivation to complete a college degree.

ANALYZING YOUR INTERNAL MOTIVATION

Answer the following questions to get a better idea of your internal motivation for your chosen major.

How will this major be fun for you to study?

_____

_____

How will this major help you contribute to society?

_____

_____

How does this major help you to be in charge of your own fate?

_____

_____

How will this major allow you to be either critical or creative?

_____

_____

What talents do you possess that this major will allow you to use?

_____

_____

ANALYZING YOUR EXTERNAL MOTIVATION

Answer the following questions to get a better idea of your external motivation for your chosen major.

How will this major make you in demand by prospective employers?

_____

_____

How will this major lead to a job where you can develop the lifestyle you desire?

_____

_____

What options will this major provide beyond a job after college?

_____

_____

What transferable skills will this major provide?

_____

_____

What security (in terms of pay and benefits for related occupations) does this major provide?

_____

_____

Goal Attainment

Whether you believe it or not, you probably are already formulating goals in your mind to reality test your decision about a major. An important aspect of making a final decision about the college major you want to declare, *reality testing* is the process by which you explore and integrate aspects of both the internal and external worlds. Reality testing occurs when you begin to see the connection between the two major types of motivation and begin to plan for both. For example, as you develop an action plan, you might think about how the major will be fun and allow you to utilize your creative imagination as well as be profitable in the future.

CREATING AN ACTION PLAN

Based on your work in this book, you now have an idea of the best major(s) for you on campus. You now need to develop goals that will motivate you to meet your ultimate goal of earning a college degree in that major. In order to achieve your goals, it is important to develop an action plan by following the steps outlined here.

Step 1: Focus on what's important. Now that you have chosen a major, what is important for you to do?

_____

_____

_____

Step 2: Commit to your goal. How will you begin committing to your new major?

_____

_____

_____

Step 3: Track your progress. How will you know that you made the right decision?

_____

_____

_____

The following sections provide some tips for developing, writing, and sticking to your goals.

Break Larger Goals into Smaller Ones

Maintaining goal motivation is important as you reality test your decisions about college majors of interest. To maintain goal motivation, set goals that are achievable in the time frame that you identify. By breaking your goals into time frames, you will achieve them much more easily and you will not get overwhelmed by all that you must accomplish. Although goals fall into varying time periods, there are three generally accepted time frames that are used when setting goals:

- Short-term goals are those you want to achieve within the next six months.

- Medium-range goals are those you want to achieve within 6 to 12 months.

- Long-term goals are those you want to achieve after a year or more.

SETTING TIME FRAMES FOR GOALS

Write five short-term, medium-range, and long-term goals that are related to your college major choice.

Short-Term Goals	Medium-Range Goals	Long-Term Goals
_____	_____	_____
_____	_____	_____
_____	_____	_____
_____	_____	_____
_____	_____	_____

Be Positive

You are much more likely to achieve goals if you write them down. The act of writing goals down enhances your commitment to them. Experts believe that the more you see your goals written out, the more they will be imprinted on your brain. When you write down your goals, be sure to state them in a positive manner, as in the following examples:

> Short-term goal: "I will talk with the academic advisor in the math department next week."

> Medium-range: "I will join the History Club on campus next semester to learn more about history."

> Long-term goal: "I will volunteer in the art museum next summer."

WRITING GOAL STATEMENTS

Choose one goal for each time frame from the previous worksheet and write it in a positive statement:

Short-term goal: _____

Medium-range goal: _____

Long-term goal: _____

Prioritize

Because you have a limited amount of time and energy, you must begin to prioritize the tasks that will help you choose a major. Prioritizing is the process by which you organize tasks that are important to you and give those tasks more of your immediate time, attention, and energy. When you prioritize, you identify and focus on what is most important at the expense of tasks that can be attended to at a later time. The most important, or high priority, tasks are the tasks that will lead to the greatest success in the smallest amount of time. The worksheet that follows is designed to help you begin to prioritize your goals related to choosing a major.

RANKING GOALS

Prioritize the goals you set in the Setting Time Frames for Goals worksheet from the most important to the least important within each of the three time frames (short-term, medium-range, and long-term).

Short-Term Goals	Medium-Range Goals	Long-Term Goals
1. _____	1. _____	1. _____
2. _____	2. _____	2. _____
3. _____	3. _____	3. _____
4. _____	4. _____	4. _____
5. _____	5. _____	5. _____

Take Immediate and Consistent Action

As quickly as possible, you should take some action toward one of your goals. Then take an action each day toward another one of your goals until you have achieved what you desire. Remember that the more goals you achieve, the more motivated you will become. Keep in mind that goal setting never ends. You may need to create new goals as you achieve old ones or revise goals that are no longer applicable.

DECIDING A COURSE OF ACTION

Answer the following questions:

What is it going to take to graduate with the major you have chosen?

_____

_____

What are the benefits of graduating with this major?

_____

_____

What would you like to accomplish immediately?

_____

_____

How will you accomplish this?

_____

_____

As the force that drives you to set and achieve goals in your life and career, motivation is critical in the process of choosing a major. The goal-setting activities in this chapter were designed to help you decide on and implement your choice of a college major in a way that harnesses both motivation based on internal, intrinsic satisfaction and motivation based on extrinsic, material success. If you need more information to help you with your college major decision, the following appendix provides descriptions of popular college majors organized by career cluster so that you can easily explore majors that match your interests.

College Major Descriptions

Congratulations! You have completed all of the assessments in this book, made some tentative choices about a college major, and begun to develop a plan for implementing your decision. You are to be commended. Successfully choosing and implementing a college major is a lot of work.

In Part 2 of this book, you completed a variety of quizzes that helped you to explore your interests, skills, and courses you enjoyed in high school. If you look back to those sections, you will see that you received scores that were grouped into 16 clusters identified by the U.S. Department of Education. Following is a list of majors tied to each of the 16 clusters from Part 2. You can use this section to expand your knowledge of majors in clusters of interest to you and to help you identify a major at your college.

These descriptions of majors are taken from the Classification of Instructional Programs, which was developed by the U.S. Department of Education's National Center for Educational Statistics. As you go through this list of majors, please remember that all colleges will not have each of these majors. You should find the major at your college that is as close to ones of interest as possible. Also note that every possible major for each of the 16 clusters may not be represented.

Agriculture and Natural Resources

This career cluster includes majors that appeal to students with an interest in working with plants, animals, forests, or mineral resources for agriculture, horticulture, conservation, and other purposes.

Agribusiness/Agricultural Business Operations: A program that prepares individuals to manage agricultural businesses and agriculturally related operations within diversified corporations. Includes instruction in agriculture, agricultural specialization, business management, accounting, finance, marketing, planning, human resources management, and other managerial responsibilities.

Agricultural and Extension Education Services: A program that prepares individuals to provide referral, consulting, technical assistance, and educational services to gardeners, farmers, ranchers, agribusinesses, and other organizations. Includes instruction in basic agricultural sciences, agricultural business operations, pest control, adult education methods, public relations, applicable state laws and regulations, and communication skills.

Agricultural Animal Breeding: A program that focuses on the application of genetics and genetic engineering to the improvement of agricultural animal health, the development of new animal breeds, and the selective improvement of agricultural animal populations. Includes instruction in genetics, genetic engineering, population genetics, animal health, animal husbandry, and biotechnology.

Agricultural Business Technology: A program that prepares individuals to perform specialized support functions related to agricultural business offices and operations and to operate agricultural office equipment, software, and information systems. Includes instruction in basic agricultural business principles, office management, equipment operation, standard software, and database management.

Agricultural Communication/Journalism: A program that prepares individuals to apply journalistic, communication, and broadcasting principles to the development, production, and transmittal of agricultural information. Includes instruction in basic journalism, broadcasting, film/video, and communication techniques; the production of technically specialized information products for agricultural audiences; and the principles of agricultural sciences and business operations needed to develop and communicate agricultural subject matter in effective ways.

Agricultural Economics: A program that focuses on the application of economics to the analysis of resource allocation, productivity, investment, and trends in the agricultural sector, both domestically and internationally. Includes instruction in economics and related subfields as well as applicable agricultural fields.

Agricultural/Farm Supplies Retailing and Wholesaling: A program that prepares individuals to sell agricultural products and supplies, provide support services to agricultural enterprises, and purchase and market agricultural products. Includes instruction in basic business management, marketing, retailing and wholesaling operations, and applicable principles of agriculture and agricultural operations.

Agricultural Mechanization: A program that generally prepares individuals to sell, select, and service agricultural or agribusiness technical equipment and facilities, including computers, specialized software, power units, machinery, equipment structures, and utilities. Includes instruction in agricultural power systems; planning and selecting materials for the construction of support facilities; mechanical practices associated with irrigation and water conservation; erosion control; and agricultural data processing systems.

Agriculture: A program that focuses on the general principles and practice of agricultural research and production and that may prepare individuals to apply this knowledge to the solution of practical agricultural problems. Includes instruction in basic animal, plant, and soil science; animal husbandry and plant cultivation; soil conservation; and agricultural operations such as farming, ranching, and agricultural business.

Agronomy and Crop Science: A program that focuses on the chemical, physical, and biological relationships of crops and the soils nurturing them. Includes instruction in the growth and behavior of agricultural crops, the development of new plant varieties, and the scientific management of soils and nutrients for maximum plant nutrition, health, and productivity.

Animal Health: A program that focuses on the application of biological and chemical principles to the study, prevention, and control of diseases in agricultural animal populations. Includes instruction in environmental science, pharmacology, animal population studies, genetics, animal physiology and diet, disease prevention, treatment methodologies, and laboratory and testing procedures.

Animal Nutrition: A program that focuses on the biology and chemistry of proteins, fats, carbohydrates, water, vitamins, and feed additives as related to animal health and the production of improved animal products. Includes instruction in nutrition science, animal health and physiology, biochemistry, cellular and molecular biology, animal husbandry, and food science.

Animal Sciences: A general program that focuses on the scientific principles that underlie the breeding and husbandry of agricultural animals, and the production, processing, and distribution of agricultural animal products. Includes instruction in the animal sciences, animal husbandry and production, and agricultural and food products processing.

Aquaculture: A program that prepares individuals to select, culture, propagate, harvest, and market domesticated fish, shellfish, and marine plants, both freshwater and saltwater. Includes instruction in the basic principles of aquatic and marine biology; health and nutrition of aquatic and marine life; design and operation of fish farms, breeding facilities, culture beds, and related enterprises; and related issues of safety, applicable regulations, logistics, and supply.

Crop Production: A program that prepares individuals to cultivate grain, fiber, forage, oilseed, fruits and nuts, vegetables, and other domesticated plant products. Includes instruction in basic principles of plant science, health, and nutrition as applied to particular species and breeds; soil preparation and irrigation; pest management; planting and harvesting operations; product marketing; and applicable issues of safety, regulation, logistics, and supply.

Dairy Science: A program that focuses on the application of biological and chemical principles to the production and management of dairy animals and the production and handling of dairy products. Includes instruction in animal sciences, nutrition sciences, food science and technology, biochemistry, and related aspects of human and animal health and safety.

Environmental Science: A program that focuses on the application of biological, chemical, and physical principles to the study of the physical environment and the solution of environmental problems, including subjects such as abating or controlling environmental pollution and degradation; the interaction between human society and the natural environment; and natural resources

management. Includes instruction in biology, chemistry, physics, geosciences, climatology, statistics, and mathematical modeling.

Equestrian/Equine Studies: A program that focuses on the horse, horsemanship, and related subjects and prepares individuals to care for horses and horse equipment; ride and drive horses for leisure, sport, show, and professional purposes; and manage the training of horses and riders. Includes instruction in horse breeding, nutrition, health, and safety; history of the horse and horsemanship; horse development and training; riding and equestrian technique; stable, paddock, and track management; and equipment maintenance and repair.

Farm and Ranch Management: A program that prepares individuals to manage farms, ranches, and similar enterprises. Includes instruction in applicable agricultural specialization, business management, accounting, taxation, capitalization, purchasing, government programs and regulations, operational planning and budgeting, contracts and negotiation, and estate planning.

Fishing and Fisheries Sciences and Management: A program that focuses on the scientific study of the husbandry and production of nondomesticated fish and shellfish populations for recreational and commercial purposes and the management of fishing and marine/aquatic product processing to ensure adequate conservation and efficient utilization. Includes instruction in the principles of marine/aquatic biology, freshwater and saltwater ecosystems, water resources, fishing production operations and management, fishing policy and regulation, and the management of recreational and commercial fishing activities.

Floriculture/Floristry Operations and Management: A program that prepares individuals to operate and manage commercial and contract florist enterprises, supply and delivery services, and flower catering services. Includes instruction in principles of plant science; purchasing, storage, and delivery systems; floral design and arranging; and principles of business management.

Food Science: A program that focuses on the application of biological, chemical, and physical principles to the study of converting raw agricultural products into processed forms suitable for direct human consumption, and the storage of such products. Includes instruction in applicable aspects of the agricultural sciences, human physiology and nutrition, food chemistry, agricultural products processing, food additives, food preparation and packaging, food storage and shipment, and related aspects of human health and safety including toxicology and pathology.

Food Technology and Processing: A program that focuses on the application of chemical, physical, and engineering principles to the development and implementation of manufacturing, packaging, storage, and distribution technologies and processes for food products. Includes instruction in food engineering, preservation and handling, preparation, packaging and display, and storage and shipment, and related equipment and facilities design, operation, and maintenance.

Forest Sciences and Biology: A program that focuses on the application of one or more forest-related sciences to the study of environmental factors affecting forests and the growth and management of forest resources. Includes instruction in forest biology, forest hydrology, forest mensuration, silviculture, forest soils, water resources, environmental science, forest resources management, and wood science.

Forestry: A program that generally prepares individuals to manage and develop forest areas for economic, recreational, and ecological purposes. Includes instruction in forest-related sciences, mapping, statistics, harvesting and production technology, natural resources management and economics, wildlife sciences, administration, and public relations.

Greenhouse Operations and Management: A program that prepares individuals to produce, store, and deliver plant species in controlled indoor environments for wholesale, commercial, research, or other purposes. Includes instruction in applicable principles of plant science; climate, irrigation, and nutrition control equipment operation and maintenance; facilities management; inventory control; safety procedures; and personnel supervision.

Horse Husbandry/Equine Science and Management: A program that prepares individuals to manage the selection, breeding, care, and maintenance of work, athletic, and show horses; and horse farms, stables, tracks, and related equipment and operations. Includes instruction in applicable principles of animal science, care, and health; stable and track management; design and operation of facilities and equipment; and related issues such as regulations, business management, and logistics.

Horticultural Science: A program that focuses on the scientific principles related to the cultivation of garden and ornamental plants, including fruits, vegetables, flowers, and landscape and nursery crops. Includes instruction in specific types of plants, such as citrus; breeding horticultural varieties; physiology of horticultural species; and the scientific management of horticultural plant development and production through the life cycle.

International Agriculture: A program that focuses on the application of agricultural management and scientific principles to the problems of global food production and distribution, and to the study of the agricultural systems of other countries. Includes instruction in agricultural economics; comparative agricultural systems; international agribusiness and law; third-world development studies and economic development; and global applications of climate, soil, water resources, ecological and environmental studies, and animal and plant sciences.

Land Use Planning and Management/Development: A program that focuses on how public and/or private land and associated resources can be preserved, developed, and used for maximum social, economic, and environmental benefit. Includes instruction in natural resources management, natural resource economics, public policy, regional and land use planning, environmental impact assessment, applicable law and regulations, government and politics, principles of business and real estate land use, statistical and analytical tools, computer applications, mapping and report preparation, site analysis, cost analysis, and communications skills.

Livestock Management: A program that focuses on the application of biological and chemical principles to the production and management of livestock animals and the production and handling of meat and other products. Includes instruction in animal sciences, range science, nutrition sciences, food science and technology, biochemistry, and related aspects of human and animal health and safety.

Natural Resource Economics: A program that focuses on the application of economic concepts and methods to the analysis of issues such as air and water pollution, land use planning, waste disposal, invasive species and pest control, conservation policies, and related environmental problems. Includes instruction in cost-benefit analysis; environmental impact assessment; evaluation and assessment of alternative resource management strategies; policy evaluation and monitoring; and descriptive and analytic tools for studying how environmental developments affect the economic system.

Natural Resources/Conservation: A general program that focuses on the studies and activities relating to the natural environment and its conservation, use, and improvement. Includes instruction in subjects such as climate, air, soil, water, land, fish and wildlife, and plant resources; in the basic principles of environmental science and natural resources management; and the recreational and economic uses of renewable and nonrenewable natural resources.

Plant Nursery Operations and Management: A program that prepares individuals to operate and manage outdoor plant farms, tree and shrub nurseries, and related facilities that develop domesticated plant products for propagation, harvesting, and transplantation. Includes instruction in applicable principles of plant science, farm and business management, nursery operations, equipment operation and maintenance, safety procedures, and personnel supervision.

Plant Protection and Integrated Pest Management: A program that focuses on the application of scientific principles to the control of animal and weed infestation of domesticated plant populations, including agricultural crops; the prevention/reduction of attendant economic loss; and the control of environmental pollution and degradation related to pest infestation and pest control measures. Includes instruction in entomology, applicable animal sciences, plant pathology and physiology, weed science, crop science, and environmental toxicology.

Plant Sciences: A general program that focuses on the scientific principles that underlie the breeding, cultivation, and production of agricultural plants and the production, processing, and distribution of agricultural plant products. Includes instruction in the plant sciences, crop cultivation and production, and agricultural and food products processing.

Poultry Science: A program that focuses on the application of biological and chemical principles to the production and management of poultry animals and the production and handling of poultry products. Includes instruction in avian sciences, nutrition sciences, food science and technology, biochemistry, hatchery design, and related aspects of human and animal health and safety.

Range Science and Management: A program that focuses on the scientific study of rangelands, arid regions, grasslands, and other areas of low productivity, as well as the principles of managing such resources for maximum benefit and environmental balance. Includes instruction in livestock management, wildlife biology, plant sciences, ecology, soil science, and hydrology.

Soil Chemistry and Physics: A program that focuses on the application of chemical and physical principles to research and analysis concerning the nature and properties of soils and the conservation and management of soils. Includes instruction in soil and fluid mechanics, mineralogy, sedimentology, thermodynamics, geomorphology, environmental systems, analytical methods, and organic and inorganic chemistry.

Soil Science and Agronomy: A program that generally focuses on the scientific classification of soils, soil properties, and their relationship to agricultural crops. Includes instruction in soil chemistry, soil physics, soil biology, soil fertility, morphogenesis, mineralogy, hydrology, agronomy, and soil conservation and management.

Turf and Turfgrass Management: A program that focuses on turfgrasses and related groundcover plants and prepares individuals to develop ornamental or recreational grasses and related products; plant, transplant, and manage grassed areas; and to produce and store turf used for transplantation. Includes instruction in applicable plant sciences, genetics of grasses, turf science, use analysis, turf management, and related economics.

Water, Wetlands, and Marine Resources Management: A program that prepares individuals to apply the principles of marine/aquatic biology, oceanography, natural resource economics, and natural resources management to the development, conservation, and management of freshwater and saltwater environments. Includes instruction in subjects such as wetland, riverine, lacustrine, coastal, and oceanic water resources; water conservation and use; flood control; pollution control; water supply logistics; wastewater management; aquatic and marine ecology; aquatic and marine life conservation; and the economic and recreational uses of water resources.

Wildlife and Wildlands Science and Management: A program that prepares individuals to conserve and manage wilderness areas and the flora and fauna therein and manage wildlife reservations and zoological facilities for recreational, commercial, and ecological purposes. Includes instruction in wildlife biology, environmental science, natural resources management and policy, outdoor recreation and parks management, the design and operation of natural and artificial wildlife habitats, applicable law and regulations, and related administrative and communications skills.

Wood Science and Wood Products/Pulp and Paper Technology: A program that focuses on the application of chemical, physical, and engineering principles to the analysis of the properties and behavior of wood and wood products and the development of processes for converting wood into paper and other products. Includes instruction in wood classification and testing, product development, manufacturing and processing technologies, and the design and development of related equipment and systems.

Architecture and Construction

This career cluster includes majors that appeal to students with an interest in designing, assembling, and maintaining buildings and other structures.

Architectural History and Criticism: A general program that focuses on the aesthetic, technical, and social development of the built environment and the architectural profession from earliest times to the present. Includes instruction in the principles of architecture and related fields; art history; historiography of architecture; architectural theory and criticism; related aspects of the history of technology and social and economic history; and various period, cultural, and stylistic specializations.

Architectural Technology: A program that prepares individuals to assist architects in developing plans and related documentation and in performing architectural office services. Includes instruction in architectural drafting, computer-assisted drafting and design, construction methods and materials, environmental systems, building codes and standards, structural principles, cost estimation, planning documentation, visual communication skills, display production, and architectural office management.

Architecture: A program that prepares individuals for the independent professional practice of architecture and to conduct research in various aspects of the field. Includes instruction in architectural design, history, and theory; building structures and environmental systems; project and site planning; construction; professional responsibilities and standards; and related cultural, social, economic, and environmental issues.

Building/Home/Construction Inspection: A program that prepares individuals to apply industrial, labor, and governmental standards and laws to the oversight of construction projects and the maintenance of completed buildings and other structures. Includes instruction in construction processes and techniques, materials analysis, occupational safety and health, industry standards, building codes and specifications, blueprint interpretation, testing equipment and procedures, communication skills, accident investigation, and documentation.

Building/Property Maintenance and Management: A program that prepares individuals to apply technical knowledge and skills to keep a building functioning, and to service a variety of structures including commercial and industrial buildings and mobile homes. Includes instruction in the basic maintenance and repair skills required to service building systems, such as air conditioning, heating, plumbing, electrical, major appliances, and other mechanical systems.

City/Urban, Community, and Regional Planning: A program that prepares individuals to apply principles of planning, analysis, and architecture to the development and improvement of urban areas and surrounding regions, and to function as professional planners. Includes instruction in principles of architecture; master plan development; service, communications, and transportation systems design; community and commercial development; zoning; land use planning; applied economics; policy analysis; applicable laws and regulations; and professional responsibilities and managerial duties.

Construction Management: A program that prepares individuals to manage, coordinate, and supervise the construction process from concept development through project completion on timely and economic bases. Includes instruction in commercial, residential, mechanical, highway/heavy civil, electrical, environmental, industrial, and specialty construction; facilities management; project planning; budgeting and cost control; logistics and materials management; personnel management and labor relations; site safety; construction contracting; construction processes and techniques; organization and scheduling; and applicable codes and regulations.

Construction Trades: A program that generally prepares individuals to apply technical knowledge and skills in the building, inspecting, and maintaining of structures and related properties. May include instruction in masonry, carpentry, electrical and power transmission installation, building/construction finishing, management, inspection, and other construction-related applications.

Electrician: A program that prepares individuals to apply technical knowledge and skills to install, operate, maintain, and repair electric apparatus and systems such as residential, commercial, and industrial electric-power wiring; and DC and AC motors, controls, and electrical distribution panels. Includes instruction in the principles of electronics and electrical systems, wiring, power transmission, safety, industrial and household appliances, job estimation, electrical testing and inspection, and applicable codes and standards.

Environmental Design/Architecture: A program that prepares individuals to design public and private spaces, indoor and outdoor, for leisure, recreational, commercial, and living purposes, and for professional practice as environmental designers and architects. Includes instruction in the design and planning of public and private open spaces and their relationship to buildings and other aspects of the built environment; facilities management; related aspects of interior design and architecture, landscape architecture, and urban planning; and professional responsibilities and standards.

Landscape Architecture: A program that prepares individuals for the independent professional practice of landscape architecture and research in various aspects of the field. Includes instruction in geology and hydrology; soils, groundcovers, and horticultural elements; project and site planning; landscape design, history, and theory; environmental design; applicable law and regulations; and professional responsibilities and standards.

Plumbing Technology: A program that prepares individuals to practice as licensed plumbers by applying technical knowledge and skills to lay out, assemble, install, and maintain piping fixtures and systems for steam, natural gas, oil, hot water, heating, cooling, drainage, lubricating, sprinkling, and industrial processing systems in home and business environments. Includes instruction in source determination, water distribution, waste removal, pressure adjustment, basic physics, technical mathematics, blueprint reading, pipe installation, pumps, welding and soldering, plumbing inspection, and applicable codes and standards.

Well Drilling: A program that prepares individuals to apply technical knowledge and skills to set up, maintain, repair, and operate well drilling equipment; locate, drill, construct, and develop water, gas, and oil wells; and test and monitor wells to ensure adequate flow. Includes applications to home, business, and industrial uses.

Arts and Communication

This career cluster includes majors that appeal to students with an interest in creatively expressing feelings or ideas, in communicating news or information, or in performing.

Acting: A program that prepares individuals to communicate dramatic information, ideas, moods, and feelings through the achievement of naturalistic and believable behavior in imaginary circumstances. Includes instruction in voice and acting speech, stage dialects, movement, improvisation, acting styles, theatre history, script interpretation, and actor coaching.

Advertising: A program that focuses on the creation, execution, transmission, and evaluation of commercial messages in various media intended to promote and sell products, services, and brands; and that prepares individuals to function as advertising assistants, technicians, and managers.

Includes instruction in advertising theory, marketing strategy, advertising design and production methods, campaign methods and techniques, media management, related principles of business management, and applicable technical and equipment skills.

Animation, Interactive Technology, Video Graphics, and Special Effects: A program that prepares individuals to use computer applications and related visual and sound imaging techniques to manipulate images and information originating as film, video, still photographs, digital copy, soundtracks, and physical objects in order to communicate messages simulating real-world content. Includes instruction in specialized camerawork and equipment operation and maintenance, image capture, computer programming, dubbing, CAD applications, and applications to specific commercial, industrial, and entertainment needs.

Art/Art Studies: A general program that focuses on the introductory study and appreciation of the visual arts. Includes instruction in art, photography, and other visual communications media.

Arts Management: A program that prepares individuals to organize and manage art organizations, operations, and facilities. Includes instruction in business and financial management; marketing and fund-raising; personnel management and labor relations; event promotion and management; public relations and arts advocacy; arts law; and applications to specific arts activities such as galleries, museums, studios, foundations, and community organizations.

Broadcast Journalism: A program that focuses on the methods and techniques for reporting, producing, and delivering news and news programs via radio, television, and video/film media; and that prepares individuals to be professional broadcast journalists, editors, producers, directors, and managers. Includes instruction in the principles of broadcast technology; broadcast reporting; on- and off-camera and microphone procedures and techniques; program, sound, and video/film editing; program design and production; media law and policy; and professional standards and ethics.

Ceramic Arts and Ceramics: A program that prepares individuals creatively and technically to express emotions, ideas, or inner visions by producing art works out of clay and similar materials. Includes instruction in hand-built and wheel-thrown techniques; molding; slips and glazes; trimming and decorating; firing and kiln operation; oxidation; mixed media; ceramic murals, and personal style development.

Cinematography and Film/Video Production: A program that prepares individuals to communicate dramatic information, ideas, moods, and feelings through the making and producing of films and videos. Includes instruction in theory of film; film technology and equipment operation; film production; film directing; film editing; cinematographic art; film audio; techniques for making specific types of films and/or videos; the use of computer applications to record or enhance images, audio, or effects; and the planning and management of film/video operations.

Commercial and Advertising Art: A program in the applied visual arts that prepares individuals to use artistic techniques to effectively communicate ideas and information to business and consumer audiences via illustrations and other forms of digital or printed media. Includes instruction in concept design; layout; paste-up; and techniques such as engraving, etching, silkscreen, lithography, offset, drawing and cartooning, painting, collage, and computer graphics.

Communication Studies/Speech Communication and Rhetoric: A program that focuses on the scientific, humanistic, and critical study of human communication in a variety of formats, media, and contexts. Includes instruction in the theory and practice of interpersonal, group, organizational, professional, and intercultural communication; speaking and listening; verbal and nonverbal interaction; rhetorical theory and criticism; performance studies; argumentation and persuasion; technologically mediated communication; popular culture; and various contextual applications.

Conducting: A program that prepares individuals to master the art of leading bands, choirs, orchestras, and other ensembles in performance and related music leadership. Includes instruction in score analysis and arranging, rehearsal and performance leadership, music coaching, arrangement and performance planning, ensemble operations management, and applications to specific school or professional ensembles.

Dance: A general program that prepares individuals to express ideas, feelings, and/or inner visions through the performance of one or more of the dance disciplines, including but not limited to ballet, modern, jazz, ethnic, and folk dance, and that focuses on the study and analysis of dance as a cultural phenomenon. Includes instruction in technique, choreography, labanotation, dance history and criticism, and dance production.

Design and Visual Communications: A program in the applied visual arts that focuses on the general principles and techniques for effectively communicating ideas and information, and packaging products, in digital and other formats to business and consumer audiences and that may prepare individuals in any of the applied art media.

Digital Communication and Media/Multimedia: A program that focuses on the development, use, and regulation of new electronic communication technologies using computer applications and that prepares individuals to function as developers and managers of digital communications media. Includes instruction in the principles of computers and telecommunications technologies and processes; design and development of digital communications; marketing and distribution; digital communications regulation, law, and policy; the study of human interaction with, and use of, digital media; and emerging trends and issues.

Directing and Theatrical Production: A program that prepares individuals to manage the planning, design, preparation, and production of plays and other theatrical entertainment programs. Includes instruction in theatrical design, program management, dramatic production, rehearsal management, personnel management and casting, actor coaching, directing concepts and techniques, theatre history, scene work, script interpretation, business management, marketing, public relations, and communications skills.

Drama and Dramatics/Theatre Arts: A program that focuses on the general study of dramatic works and their performance. Includes instruction in major works of dramatic literature, dramatic styles and types, and the principles of organizing and producing full live or filmed productions.

Drawing: A program that prepares individuals creatively and technically to express emotions, ideas, or inner visions through representation by lines made on a surface. Includes instruction in eye-hand coordination; line, value, shape, and perspective; figure and still life drawing; the use of media such as pen and ink, pencil, charcoal, pastel, and brush; and personal style development.

Fashion/Apparel Design: A program that prepares individuals to apply artistic principles and techniques to the professional design of commercial fashions, apparel, and accessories, and the management of fashion development projects. Includes instruction in apparel design; accessory design; the design of men's, women's, and children's wear; flat pattern design; computer-assisted design and manufacturing; concept planning; designing in specific materials; labor and cost analysis; history of fashion; fabric art and printing; and the principles of management and operations in the fashion industry.

Fiber, Textile, and Weaving Arts: A program that prepares individuals creatively and technically to express emotions, ideas, or inner visions by constructing art works from woven or nonwoven fabrics and fibrous materials. Includes instruction in weaving techniques and loom operation; nonwoven techniques such as knitting, coiling, netting, and crocheting; quilting; dyeing and pigmentation; printing and other finishing techniques; pattern design; tapestry; and personal style development.

Film/Cinema Studies: A program in the visual arts that focuses on the study of the history, development, theory, and criticism of the film/video arts, as well as the basic principles of film making and film production.

Fine/Studio Arts: A program that prepares individuals to generally function as creative artists in the visual and plastic media. Includes instruction in the traditional fine arts media (drawing, painting, sculpture, printmaking, CAD/CAM) and/or modern media (ceramics, textiles, intermedia, photography, digital images); theory of art; color theory; composition and perspective; anatomy; the techniques and procedures for maintaining equipment and managing a studio; and art portfolio marketing.

Graphic Communications: A program that generally prepares individuals to apply technical knowledge and skills in the manufacture and distribution or transmission of graphic communications products. Includes instruction in the prepress, press, and postpress phases of production operations and processes such as offset lithography, flexography, gravure, letterpress, screen printing, foil stamping, digital imaging, and other reproduction methods.

Graphic Design: A program that prepares individuals to apply artistic and computer techniques to the interpretation of technical and commercial concepts. Includes instruction in computer-assisted art and design, printmaking, concepts sketching, technical drawing, color theory, imaging, studio technique, still and life modeling, communication skills, and commercial art business operations.

Illustration: A program that prepares individuals to use artistic techniques to develop and execute interpretations of the concepts of authors and designers to specifications. Includes instruction in book illustration, fashion illustration, map illustration, rendering, exhibit preparation, textual layout, cartooning, and the use of various artistic techniques as requested by clients.

Industrial Design: A program in the applied visual arts that prepares individuals to use artistic techniques to effectively communicate ideas and information to business and consumer audiences via the creation of effective forms, shapes, and packaging for manufactured products. Includes instruction in designing in a wide variety of plastic and digital media, prototype construction, design development and refinement, principles of cost saving, and product structure and performance criteria relevant to aesthetic design parameters.

Interior Design: A program in the applied visual arts that prepares individuals to apply artistic principles and techniques to the professional planning, designing, equipping, and furnishing of residential and commercial interior spaces. Includes instruction in computer applications drafting and graphic techniques; principles of interior lighting, acoustics, systems integration, and color coordination; furniture and furnishings; textiles and their finishing; the history of interior design and period styles; basic structural design; building codes and inspection regulations; and applications to office, hotel, factory, restaurant, and housing design.

Jazz/Jazz Studies: A program that prepares individuals to study and master the performance and composition of jazz. Includes instruction in the history of jazz and related musical styles such as the blues, jazz composition and theory, improvisation, jazz instrument and ensemble performance, and related topics.

Journalism: A program that focuses on the theory and practice of gathering, processing, and delivering news and that prepares individuals to be professional print journalists, news editors, and news managers. Includes instruction in news writing and editing; reporting; photojournalism; layout and graphic design; journalism law and policy; professional standards and ethics; research methods; and journalism history and criticism.

Mass Communication/Media Studies: A program that focuses on the analysis and criticism of media institutions and media texts, how people experience and understand media content, and the roles of media in producing and transforming culture. Includes instruction in communications regulation, law, and policy; media history; media aesthetics, interpretation, and criticism; the social and cultural effects of mass media; cultural studies; the economics of media industries; visual and media literacy; and the psychology and behavioral aspects of media messages, interpretation, and utilization.

Metal and Jewelry Arts: A program that prepares individuals creatively and technically to express emotions, ideas, or inner visions by fashioning art works from gems, other stones, and precious metals. Includes instruction in gemology; metalsmithing and finishing; stone cutting and polishing; metal and nonmetal casting and molding; electroforming; metal coloring; enameling; photo etching; lapidary technique and art; design concepts; and personal style development.

Music: A general program that focuses on the introductory study and appreciation of music and the performing arts. Includes instruction in music, dance, and other performing arts media.

Music History, Literature, and Theory: A program that focuses on the study of the historical evolution of music as a social and intellectual phenomenon, the development of musical instruments and techniques, and the analysis and criticism of musical literature. Includes instruction in music history research methods; aesthetic analysis of musical compositions; history of musical writing and notation; the development of musical instruments; the development of music theory; and the study of specific periods, cultural traditions, styles, and themes.

Music Pedagogy: A program that prepares individuals to provide musical instruction and tutoring to clients in private and institutional settings. Includes instruction in music theory, music composition, mastery of one or more instruments, familiarity with various musical genres and styles, principles of music education, and client communications.

Music Performance: A program that generally prepares individuals to master musical instruments and performing art as solo and/or ensemble performers. Includes instruction on one or more specific instruments from various instrumental groupings.

Painting: A program that prepares individuals creatively and technically to express emotions, ideas, or inner visions by the application of paints and related chemical color substances to canvases or other materials. Includes instruction in color and color mixing; surface preparation; composition; oil and acrylic media; watercolor media; painting techniques; and personal style development.

Photography: A program that focuses on the principles and techniques of communicating information, ideas, moods, and feelings through the creation of images on photographic film, plates, and digital images and that may prepare individuals to be professional photographic artists. Includes instruction in camera and equipment operation and maintenance, film and plate developing, light and composition, films and printing media, color and special effects, photographic art, photographic history, use of computer applications to record or enhance images, and applications to the photography of various subjects.

Photojournalism: A program that focuses on the use of still and motion photography in journalism and prepares individuals to function as news photographers and photographic editors. Includes instruction in photography, journalism, studio procedures and techniques, camera and equipment operation and technique, news editing, print and film editing, news scene composition, subject surveillance, media law and policy, news team field operations, and professional standards and ethics.

Playwriting and Screenwriting: A program that focuses on the principles and techniques for communicating dramatic information, ideas, moods, and feelings through the composition of creative written works for the theatre and/or film. Includes instruction in creative writing craft, scene writing, script development, stage and/or camera instructions, line and moment analysis, script reading, script editing, and the creation of full productions.

Political Communication: A program that focuses on human and media communication in the political process and that prepares individuals to function as members of political and public affairs organizations, political campaign staffs, and related government and media entities. Includes instruction in media effects, political speaking and debating, political advertising and marketing, image management, political journalism, opinion polling, and aspects of print and broadcast media related to the production and distribution of media messages in political settings.

Prepress/Desktop Publishing and Digital Imaging Design: A program that prepares individuals to apply technical knowledge and skills to the layout, design, and typographic arrangement of printed and/or electronic graphic and textual products. Includes instruction in printing and lithographic equipment and operations; computer hardware and software; digital imaging; print preparation; page layout and design; desktop publishing; and applicable principles of graphic design and web page design.

Printing Management: A program that prepares individuals to apply technical and managerial knowledge and skills to the processes and procedures of managing printing operations from initial design through finished product distribution. Includes instruction in the principles of graphic

communications design and production, quality control, printing operations management, computerization, printing plant management, business finance and marketing, logistics and distribution, personnel supervision and leadership, and professional standards in the graphic communications industry.

Printmaking: A program that prepares individuals creatively and technically to express emotions, ideas, or inner visions by rendering art concepts onto surfaces and transferring images, via ink or dyes, onto paper or fabric. Includes instruction in monochrome and color printing; tonality; chemistry; equipment setup and maintenance; techniques such as serigraphy, lithography, intaglio, woodcut, block, stencil, relief, etching, and composite; and personal style development.

Public Relations/Image Management: A program that focuses on the theories and methods for managing the media image of a business, organization, or individual and the communication process with stakeholders, constituencies, audiences, and the general public; and that prepares individuals to function as public relations assistants, technicians, and managers. Includes instruction in public relations theory; related principles of advertising, marketing, and journalism; message/image design; image management; special event management; media relations; community relations; public affairs; and internal communications.

Publishing: A program that focuses on the process of managing the creation, publication, and distribution of print and electronic books and other text products and prepares individuals to manage the editorial, technical, and business aspects of publishing operations. Includes instruction in product planning and design, editing, author relations, business and copyright law, publishing industry operations, contracting and purchasing, product marketing, electronic publishing and commerce, history of publishing, and professional standards and ethics.

Radio and Television Broadcasting Technology: A program that prepares individuals to apply technical knowledge and skills to the production of radio and television programs, and related operations, under the supervision of broadcast and studio managers, directors, editors, and producers. Includes instruction in sound, lighting, and camera operation and maintenance; power and feed control; studio operations; production preparation; broadcast engineering; related computer applications; and specialized applications such as news, entertainment, live talk, sports, commercials, and taping.

Recording Arts Technology: A program that prepares individuals to apply technical knowledge and skills to the production of sound recordings as finished products or as components of film/ video, broadcast, live, or mixed media productions. Includes instruction in sound equipment operation and maintenance; music, dialog, and sound effects recording; sound track editing; dubbing and mixing; sound engineering; tape, disk, and CD production; digital recording and transmission; amplification and modulation; and working with producers, editors, directors, artists, and production managers.

Sculpture: A program that prepares individuals creatively and technically to express emotions, ideas, or inner visions by creating three-dimensional art works. Includes instruction in the analysis of form in space; round and relief concepts; sculptural composition; modern and experimental methods; different media such as clay, plaster, wood, stone, and metal; techniques such as carving, molding, welding, casting, and modeling; and personal style development.

Technical Theatre/Theatre Design and Technology: A program that prepares individuals to apply artistic, technical, and dramatic principles and techniques to the communication of dramatic information, ideas, moods, and feelings through technical theatre methods. Includes instruction in set design, lighting design, sound effects, theatre acoustics, scene painting, property management, costume design, and technical direction and production and use of computer applications to support these functions.

Theatre/Theatre Arts Management: A program that prepares individuals to apply business management principles to the management of theatres and production corporations. Includes instruction in theatrical production, theatre design and planning, fund-raising and promotion, investment strategies, human resources management, theatre operations management, marketing, public relations, financial management and insurance, and applicable laws and regulations.

Business and Administration

This career cluster includes majors that appeal to students with an interest in making an organization run smoothly.

Accounting: A program that prepares individuals to practice the profession of accounting and to perform related business functions. Includes instruction in accounting principles and theory; financial accounting; managerial accounting; cost accounting; budget control; tax accounting; legal aspects of accounting; auditing; reporting procedures; statement analysis; planning and consulting; business information systems; accounting research methods; professional standards and ethics; and applications to specific for-profit, public, and nonprofit organizations.

Auditing: A program that prepares individuals, including certified accountants, to perform independent internal and external appraisals to evaluate organizational financial and operational activities, ensure compliance with laws and policies, safeguard assets, and promote effective planning and resource allocation. Includes instruction in advanced accounting, audit tools and techniques, sampling, risk and control, audit planning, audit function management, law and regulations, environmental auditing, information technology applications, professional standards and ethics, and specific industry and service sector problems.

Business Administration and Management: A program that generally prepares individuals to plan, organize, direct, and control the functions and processes of a firm or organization. Includes instruction in management theory, human resources management and behavior, accounting and other quantitative methods, purchasing and logistics, organization and production, marketing, and business decision making.

Business/Commerce: A program that focuses on the general study of business, including the processes of interchanging goods and services (buying, selling, and producing), business organization, and accounting as used in profit-making and nonprofit public and private institutions and agencies. The programs may prepare individuals to apply business principles and techniques in various occupational settings.

Business/Corporate Communications: A program that prepares individuals to function in an organization as a composer, editor, and proofreader of business-related communications.

Business/Managerial Economics: A program that focuses on the application of economics principles to the analysis of the organization and operation of business enterprises. Includes instruction in monetary theory, banking and financial systems, theory of competition, pricing theory, wage and salary/incentive theory, analysis of markets, and applications of econometrics and quantitative methods to the study of particular businesses and business problems.

Business Statistics: A program that focuses on the application of mathematical statistics to the description, analysis, and forecasting of business data. Includes instruction in statistical theory and methods, computer applications, data analysis and display, long- and short-term forecasting methods, and market performance analysis.

Customer Service Management: A program that prepares individuals to supervise and monitor customer service performance and manage frontline customer support services, call centers/help desks, and customer relations. Includes instruction in customer behavior, specialized information technology and systems management, developing and using customer service databases, user surveys and other feedback mechanisms, strategic and performance planning and analysis, operations management, personnel supervision, and communications and marketing skills.

E-commerce: A program that prepares individuals to plan, manage, supervise, and market electronic business operations, products, and services provided online via the Internet. Includes instruction in business administration, information technology, information resources management, web design, computer and Internet law and policy, computer privacy and security, e-trading, insurance, electronic marketing, investment capital planning, enterprise operations, personnel supervision, contracting, and product and service networking.

Entrepreneurship/Entrepreneurial Studies: A program that generally prepares individuals to perform development, marketing, and management functions associated with owning and operating a business.

Franchising and Franchise Operations: A program that prepares individuals to manage and operate franchises. Includes instruction in legal requirements, setup costs and capitalization requirements, financing, and applications to specific franchise opportunities.

Hospitality Administration/Management: A program that prepares individuals to serve as general managers and directors of hospitality operations on a systemwide basis, including both travel arrangements and promotion and the provision of traveler facilities. Includes instruction in principles of operations in the travel and tourism, hotel and lodging facilities, food services, and recreation facilities industries; hospitality marketing strategies; hospitality planning; management and coordination of franchise and unit operations; business management; accounting and financial management; hospitality transportation and logistics; and hospitality industry policies and regulations.

Human Resources Management/Personnel Administration: A program that generally prepares individuals to manage the development of human capital in organizations and to provide related services to individuals and groups. Includes instruction in personnel and organization policy, human resource dynamics and flows, labor relations, sex roles, civil rights, human resources law and regulations, motivation and compensation systems, work systems, career management, employee testing and assessment, recruitment and selection, managing employee and job training programs, and the management of human resources programs and operations.

International Business/Trade/Commerce: A program that prepares individuals to manage international businesses and/or business operations. Includes instruction in the principles and processes of export sales, trade controls, foreign operations and related problems, monetary issues, international business policy, and applications to doing business in specific countries and markets.

Labor and Industrial Relations: A program that focuses on employee-management interactions and the management of issues and disputes regarding working conditions and worker benefit packages, and that may prepare individuals to function as labor or personnel relations specialists. Includes instruction in labor history, policies and strategies of the labor movement, union organization, labor-management negotiation, labor law and contract interpretation, labor economics, welfare and benefit packages, grievance procedures, and labor policy studies.

Labor Studies: A program that focuses on the study of various aspects of work, labor organization and policy, and labor movements from the perspective of the social sciences and history. Includes instruction in labor history; political and ideological issues; worker movements and social organizations; civil rights; labor law and policy studies; labor economics; international and comparative labor studies; and applications to specific industries, groups, locations, and time periods.

Logistics and Materials Management: A program that prepares individuals to manage and coordinate all logistical functions in an enterprise, ranging from acquisitions to receiving and handling, through internal allocation of resources to operations units, to the handling and delivery of output. Includes instruction in acquisitions and purchasing, inventory control, storage and handling, just-in-time manufacturing, logistics planning, shipping and delivery management, transportation, quality control, resource estimation and allocation, and budgeting.

Management Science: A general program that focuses on the application of mathematical modeling, programming, forecasting, and operations research techniques to the analysis of problems of business organization and performance. Includes instruction in optimization theory and mathematical techniques, stochastic and dynamic modeling, operations analysis, and the design and testing of prototype systems and evaluation models.

Nonprofit/Public/Organizational Management: A program that prepares individuals to manage the business affairs of nonprofit corporations, including foundations, educational institutions, associations, and other such organizations, and public agencies and governmental operations. Includes instruction in business management, principles of public administration, principles of accounting and financial management, human resources management, taxation of nonprofit organizations, and business law as applied to nonprofit organizations.

Office Management and Supervision: A program that prepares individuals to supervise and manage the operations and personnel of business offices and management-level divisions. Includes instruction in employee supervision, management, and labor relations; budgeting; scheduling and coordination; office systems operation and maintenance; office records management, organization, and security; office facilities design and space management; preparation and evaluation of business management data; and public relations.

Operations Management and Supervision: A program that prepares individuals to manage and direct the physical and/or technical functions of a firm or organization, particularly those relating to development, production, and manufacturing. Includes instruction in principles of general management, manufacturing, and production systems; plant management; equipment maintenance management; production control; industrial labor relations and skilled trades supervision; strategic manufacturing policy; systems analysis; productivity analysis and cost control; and materials planning.

Organizational Behavior Studies: A program that focuses on the scientific study of the behavior and motivations of individuals functioning in organized groups, and its application to business and industrial settings. Includes instruction in organization theory, industrial and organizational psychology, social psychology, sociology of organizations, reinforcement and incentive theory, employee relations strategies, organizational power and influence, organization stratification and hierarchy, leadership styles, and applications of operations research and other methodologies to organizational analysis.

Parts, Warehousing, and Inventory Management Operations: A program that prepares individuals to provide administrative, technical, and managerial support in the operation of warehouses, control of inventory, parts identification, and the performance of counter services for customers. Includes instruction in record-keeping, equipment operation, database entry, supply logistics, shop operations and math, and customer and supplier relations.

Purchasing, Procurement/Acquisitions, and Contracts Management: A program that prepares individuals to manage and/or administer the processes by which a firm or organization contracts for goods and services to support its operations, as well as contracts it to sell to other firms or organizations. Includes instruction in contract law, negotiations, buying procedures, government contracting, cost and price analysis, vendor relations, contract administration, auditing and inspection, relations with other firm departments, and applications to special areas such as high-technology systems, international purchasing, and construction.

Small Business Administration/Management: A program that prepares individuals to develop and manage independent small businesses. Includes instruction in business administration; enterprise planning and entrepreneurship; startup; small business operations and problems; personnel supervision; capitalization and investment; taxation; business law and regulations; e-commerce; home business operations; and applications to specific sectors, products, and services.

Education and Training

This career cluster includes majors that appeal to students with an interest in helping people learn.

Administration of Special Education: A program that prepares individuals to plan, supervise, and manage programs for exceptional students and their parents. Includes instruction in special education theory and practice, special education program development, evaluation and assessment in special education, state and federal law and regulations, managing individual education plans, problems of low- and high-disability students, mainstreaming, special education curricula, staff management, parent education, communications and community relations, budgeting, and professional standards and ethics.

Adult and Continuing Education Administration: A program that focuses on the principles and techniques of administering programs and facilities designed to serve the basic education needs of undereducated adults, or the continuing education needs of adults seeking further or specialized instruction, and that prepares individuals to serve as administrators of such programs. Includes instruction in adult education principles, program and facilities planning, personnel management, community and client relations, budgeting and administration, professional standards, and applicable laws and policies.

Adult and Continuing Education and Teaching: A program that prepares individuals to teach adult students in various settings, including basic and remedial education programs, continuing education programs, and programs designed to develop or upgrade specific employment-related knowledge and skills.

Bilingual and Multilingual Education: A program that focuses on the design and provision of teaching and other educational services to bilingual/bicultural children or adults, and/or the design and implementation of educational programs having the goal of producing bilingual/bicultural individuals. Includes preparation to serve as teachers and administrators in bilingual/bicultural education programs.

Community College Education: A program that focuses on the principles and techniques of administering community and junior colleges and related postsecondary systems, the study of community and junior colleges as objects of applied research, and that may prepare individuals to function as administrators in such settings. Includes instruction in community and junior college finance; policy and planning studies; curriculum; faculty and labor relations; higher education law; student services; research on community and junior colleges; institutional research; marketing and promotion; and issues of evaluation, accountability, and philosophy.

Early Childhood Education and Teaching: A program that prepares individuals to teach students ranging in age from infancy through eight years (grade three), depending on the school system or state regulations. Includes preparation to teach all relevant subject matter.

Education: A program that focuses on the general theory and practice of learning and teaching, the basic principles of educational psychology, the art of teaching, the planning and administration of educational activities, school safety and health issues, and the social foundations of education.

Education/Teaching of Individuals in Early Childhood Special Education Programs: A program that focuses on the design and provision of teaching and other educational services to infant and preschool-age children with special learning needs or disabilities, and that prepares individuals to teach such students. Includes instruction in diagnosing learning disabilities, developing individual education plans, teaching and supervising special education students, special education counseling, and applicable laws and policies.

Education/Teaching of the Gifted and Talented: A program that focuses on the design of educational services for children or adults exhibiting exceptional intellectual, psychomotor, or artistic talent or potential, or who exhibit exceptional maturity or social leadership talents, and that may prepare individuals to teach such students. Includes instruction in identifying gifted and talented students, developing individual education plans, teaching and supervising gifted and talented students, counseling, and abiding by applicable laws and policies.

Educational Assessment, Testing, and Measurement: A program that focuses on the principles and procedures for designing, developing, implementing, and evaluating tests and other mechanisms used to measure learning; evaluate student progress; and assess the performance of specific teaching tools, strategies, and curricula. Includes instruction in psychometric measurement, instrument design, test implementation techniques, research evaluation, data reporting requirements, and data analysis and interpretation.

Educational Evaluation and Research: A program that focuses on the principles and procedures for generating information about educational programs, personnel, and methods, and the analysis of such information for planning purposes. Includes instruction in evaluation theory, evaluation research design and planning, evaluation administration and related data collection activities, data reporting requirements, data analysis and interpretation, and related economic and policy issues.

Educational, Instructional, and Curriculum Supervision: A program that prepares individuals to supervise instructional and support personnel at the school building, facility, or staff level. Includes instruction in the principles of staffing and organization, the supervision of learning activities, personnel relations, administrative duties related to departmental or unit management, and specific applications to various educational settings and curricula.

Educational/Instructional Media Design: A program that focuses on the principles and techniques of creating instructional products and related educational resources in various formats or combinations such as film, video, recording, text, art, CD-ROM, computer software, virtual reality technology, and three-dimensional objects, and that prepares individuals to function as instructional media designers. Includes instruction in the techniques specific to creating in various media; the behavioral principles applicable to using various media in learning and teaching; the design, testing, and production of instructional materials; and the management of educational/instructional media facilities and programs.

Elementary and Middle School Administration/Principalship: A program that focuses on educational administration at the elementary and middle school (K–7) levels and prepares individuals to serve as principals and masters of elementary and middle schools. Includes instruction in elementary and/or middle school education, program and facilities planning, budgeting and administration, public relations, human resources management, childhood and pre-adolescent growth and

development, counseling skills, applicable laws and regulations, school safety, policy studies, and professional standards and ethics.

Elementary Education and Teaching: A program that prepares individuals to teach students in the elementary grades, which may include kindergarten through grade eight, depending on the school system or state regulations. Includes preparation to teach all elementary education subject matter.

International and Comparative Education: A program that focuses on the educational phenomena, practices, and institutions within different societies and states in comparative perspective and the study of international educational issues. Includes instruction in comparative research methods, country- or area-specific studies, cross-national studies of learning and teaching styles, international educational policy and development, and analyses of educational migration patterns and experiences.

Junior High/Intermediate/Middle School Education and Teaching: A program that prepares individuals to teach students in the middle, intermediate, or junior high grades, which may include grades four through nine by regulation.

Multicultural Education: A program that focuses on the design and implementation of instructional and advising services for culturally diverse learning populations. Includes instruction in cultural diversity; at-risk populations; multilingual and ESL education; program and curriculum design; instructional technology; information resources; LEP and minority education strategies; counseling and communicating with multicultural populations; laws and regulations; and applications to specific cultural groups, educational services, and research issues.

School Librarian/School Library Media Specialist: A program that prepares individuals to serve as librarians and media specialists in elementary and secondary schools as well as special instructional centers.

Secondary Education and Teaching: A program that prepares individuals to teach students in the secondary grades, which may include grades 7 through 12, depending on the school system or state regulations. May include preparation to teach a comprehensive curriculum or specific subject matter.

Secondary School Administration/Principalship: A program that focuses on educational administration at the junior high, secondary, or senior high school (7–12) levels, and prepares individuals to serve as principals and masters of secondary schools. Includes instruction in secondary school education, program and facilities planning, budgeting and administration, public relations, human resources management, adolescent growth and development, counseling skills, applicable laws and regulations, school safety, policy studies, and professional standards and ethics.

Special Education and Teaching: A general program that focuses on the design and provision of teaching and other educational services to children or adults with special learning needs or disabilities and that may prepare individuals to function as special education teachers. Includes instruction in diagnosing learning disabilities, developing individual education plans, teaching and supervising special education students, special education counseling, and abiding by applicable laws and policies.

Finance and Insurance

This career cluster includes majors that appeal to students with an interest in helping businesses and people secure their future.

Accounting and Finance: An integrated or combined program in accounting and finance that prepares individuals to function as accountants and financial managers or analysts.

Actuarial Science: A program that focuses on the mathematical and statistical analysis of risk and their applications to insurance and other business management problems. Includes instruction in forecasting theory, quantitative and nonquantitative risk measurement methodologies, development of risk tables, secondary data analysis, and computer-assisted research methods.

Banking and Financial Support Services: A program that prepares individuals to perform a wide variety of customer services in banks, insurance agencies, savings and loan companies, and related enterprises. Includes instruction in communications and public relations skills, business equipment operation, and technical skills applicable to the methods and operations of specific financial or insurance services.

Credit Management: A program that prepares individuals to perform and/or manage operations concerning personal and corporate credit, collateral, loan processing, and related financial agency communications. Includes instruction in general finance and banking principles, insurance, real estate, taxation, business law and regulations, quantitative methods, financial computer systems applications, database management, communications skills, business and office management, and professional standards and ethics.

Finance: A program that generally prepares individuals to plan, manage, and analyze the financial and monetary aspects and performance of business enterprises, banking institutions, or other organizations. Includes instruction in principles of accounting, financial instruments, capital planning, funds acquisition, asset and debt management, budgeting, financial analysis, and investments and portfolio management.

Financial Planning and Services: A program that prepares individuals to plan and manage the financial interests and growth of individuals and institutions. Includes instruction in portfolio management, investment management, estate planning, insurance, tax planning, strategic investing and planning, financial consulting services, and client relations.

Insurance: A program that prepares individuals to manage risk in organizational settings and provide insurance and risk-aversion services to businesses, individuals, and other organizations. Includes instruction in casualty insurance and general liability, property insurance, employee benefits, social and health insurance, loss adjustment, underwriting, risk theory, and pension planning.

International Finance: A program that prepares individuals to manage international financial operations and related currency transactions. Includes instruction in international banking, international monetary and financial policy, money and capital markets, foreign exchange, risk analysis, and international cash flow operations.

Investments and Securities: A program that prepares individuals to manage assets placed in capital markets and related technical operations. Includes instruction in security analysis, debt and equity analysis, investment strategies, securities markets, computer-assisted research, portfolio management, portfolio performance analysis, and applications to specific investment problems and business situations.

Public Finance: A program that prepares individuals to manage the financial assets and budgets of public sector organizations. Includes instruction in public trusts and investments; the laws and procedures used to plan, prepare, and administer public agency budgets; and the preparation and analysis of public budget projections and policies.

Real Estate: A program that prepares individuals to develop, buy, sell, appraise, and manage real property. Includes instruction in land use development policy, real estate law, real estate marketing procedures, agency management, brokerage, property inspection and appraisal, real estate investing, leased and rental properties, commercial real estate, and property management.

Taxation: A program that prepares individuals to provide tax advice and management services to individuals and corporations. Includes instruction in tax law and regulations, tax record systems, individual and corporate income taxation, tax planning, partnerships and fiduciary relationships, estates and trusts, property depreciation, capital gains and losses, dispositions, transfers, liquidity, valuation, and applications to specific tax problems.

Government and Public Administration

This career cluster includes majors that appeal to students with an interest in helping a government agency serve the needs of the public.

Administrative Assistant and Secretarial Science: A program that generally prepares individuals to perform the duties of administrative assistants and/or secretaries and stenographers. Includes instruction in business communications, principles of business law, word processing and data entry, office machines operation and maintenance, office procedures, public relations, secretarial accounting, filing systems and records management, and report preparation.

American Government and Politics (United States): A program that focuses on the systematic study of United States political institutions and behavior. Includes instruction in American political theory, political parties and interest groups, state and local governments, Constitutional law, federalism and national institutions, executive and legislative politics, judicial politics, popular attitudes and media influences, political research methods, and applications to the study of specific issues and institutions.

American History (United States): A program that focuses on the development of American society, culture, and institutions from the pre-Columbian period to the present. Includes instruction in American historiography; American history sources and materials; historical research methods; and applications to the study of specific themes, issues, periods, and institutions.

Asian History: A program that focuses on the development of the societies, cultures, and institutions of the Asian continent from their origins to the present. Includes instruction in the

historiography of specific cultures and periods; sources and materials; historical research methods; and applications to the study of specific themes, issues, periods, and institutions.

Criminology: A program that focuses on the systematic study of crime as a sociopathological phenomenon, the behavior of criminals, and the social institutions evolved to respond to crime. Includes instruction in the theory of crime, psychological and social bases of criminal behavior, social value systems and the theory of punishment, criminal law and criminal justice systems, penology, rehabilitation and recidivism, studies of specific types of crime, social attitudes and policy, and applications to specific issues in law enforcement administration and policy.

Demography and Population Studies: A program that focuses on the systematic study of population models and population phenomena and related problems of social structure and behavior. Includes instruction in population growth, spatial distribution, mortality and fertility factors, migration, dynamic population modeling, population estimation and projection, mathematical and statistical analysis of population data, population policy studies, and applications to problems in economics and government planning.

European History: A program that focuses on the development of European society, culture, and institutions from their origins to the present. Includes instruction in European historiography, European history sources and materials, historical research methods, and applications to the study of specific themes, issues, periods, and institutions.

History: A program that focuses on the general study and interpretation of the past, including the gathering, recording, synthesizing, and criticizing of evidence and theories about past events. Includes instruction in historiography; historical research methods; studies of specific periods, issues, and cultures; and applications to areas such as historic preservation, public policy, and records administration.

History and Philosophy of Science and Technology: A program that focuses on the historical evolution of scientific theories and science applications and technologies, as well as the philosophy of science and its historical socio-economic context. Includes instruction in the concepts and methods of philosophical inquiry, historiography of science, and research methods in the history of the scientific and engineering disciplines, including mathematics.

International Development: A program that focuses on the systematic study of the economic development process and its application to the problems of specific countries and regions. Includes instruction in economic development theory; industrialization; land reform; infrastructural development; investment policy; the role of governments and business in development; international development organizations; and the study of social, health, and environmental influences on economic development.

International Relations and Affairs: A program that focuses on the systematic study of international politics and institutions and the conduct of diplomacy and foreign policy. Includes instruction in international relations theory, foreign policy analysis, national security and strategic studies, international law and organization, the comparative study of specific countries and regions, and the theory and practice of diplomacy.

Management Information Systems: A program that generally prepares individuals to provide and manage data systems and related facilities for processing and retrieving internal business information; select systems and train personnel; and respond to external data requests. Includes instruction in cost and accounting information systems, management control systems, personnel information systems, data storage and security, business systems networking, report preparation, computer facilities and equipment operation and maintenance, operator supervision and training, and management information systems policy and planning.

Political Science and Government: A general program that focuses on the systematic study of political institutions and behavior. Includes instruction in political philosophy, political theory, comparative government and politics, political parties and interest groups, public opinion, political research methods, studies of the government and politics of specific countries, and studies of specific political institutions and processes.

Sociology: A program that focuses on the systematic study of human social institutions and social relationships. Includes instruction in social theory; sociological research methods; social organization and structure; social stratification and hierarchies; dynamics of social change; family structures; social deviance and control; and applications to the study of specific social groups, social institutions, and social problems.

Urban Studies/Affairs: A program that focuses on the application of social science principles to the study of urban institutions and the forces influencing urban social and political life. Includes instruction in urban theory, the development and evolution of urban areas, urban sociology, principles of urban and social planning, and the politics and economics of urban government and services.

Health Science

This career cluster includes majors that appeal to students with an interest in helping people and animals be healthy.

Athletic Training: A program that prepares individuals to work in consultation with and under the supervision of physicians to prevent and treat sports injuries and associated conditions. Includes instruction in the identification, evaluation, and treatment of athletic injuries and illnesses; first aid and emergency care; therapeutic exercise; anatomy and physiology; exercise physiology; kinesiology and biomechanics; nutrition; sports psychology; personal and community health; knowledge of various sports and their biomechanical and physiological demands; and applicable professional standards and regulations.

Audiology and Hearing Sciences: A program that focuses on the scientific study of hearing processes and hearing loss and that prepares individuals to diagnose hearing loss and impairments, advise patients how to use their remaining hearing, and select and fit hearing aids and other devices. Includes instruction in acoustics, anatomy and physiology of hearing, hearing measurement, auditory pathology, middle and inner ear analysis, rehabilitation therapies and assistive technologies, and pediatric and other special applications.

Biology/Biological Sciences: A general program of biology at the introductory, basic level or a program in biology or the biological sciences that is undifferentiated as to title or content. Includes instruction in general biology and programs covering a variety of biological specializations.

Biomedical Sciences: A general program that focuses on the integrative scientific study of biological issues related to health and medicine, or a program in one or more of the biomedical sciences that is undifferentiated as to title. Includes instruction in any of the basic medical sciences at the research level; biological science research in biomedical faculties; and general studies encompassing a variety of the biomedical disciplines.

Chiropractic (DC): A program that prepares individuals for the independent professional practice of chiropractic, a health-care and healing system based on the application of noninvasive treatments and spinal adjustments to alleviate health problems caused by vertebral misalignments affecting bodily function as derived from the philosophy of Daniel Palmer. Includes instruction in the basic medical sciences, chiropractic theory and science, postural and spinal analysis, diagnostic radiology and ultrasound, adjustment technique, patient counseling, professional standards and ethics, and practice management.

Clinical/Medical Laboratory Technician: A program that prepares individuals, under the supervision of clinical laboratory scientists/medical technologists, to perform routine medical laboratory procedures and tests and to apply preset strategies to record and analyze data. Includes instruction in general laboratory procedures and skills; laboratory mathematics; medical computer applications; interpersonal and communications skills; and the basic principles of hematology, medical microbiology, immunohematology, immunology, clinical chemistry, and urinalysis.

Clinical Nutrition: A program that prepares individuals to apply the principles of dietetics and the biomedical and nutrition sciences to design and manage effective nutrition programs as part of clinical treatment and therapy programs, and to manage health-care facility food services. Includes instruction in human nutrition, nutrient metabolism, the role of foods and nutrition in health promotion and disease prevention, nutrition as a treatment regime, planning and directing hospital food service programs, diet and nutrition analysis and planning, supervision of food storage and preparation, special diets, client education, and professional standards and regulations.

Communication Disorders: A program that focuses on the general study of the application of biomedical, psychological, and physical principles to the study of the genesis, development, and treatment of speech, language, hearing, and cognitive communication problems caused by disease, injury, or disability. Includes instruction in language science, hearing science, speech and voice science, biology of communication, behavioral linguistics, psychology, and applications to the development of diagnostic and rehabilitative strategies and technologies.

Dental Assisting: A program that prepares individuals to provide patient care, take dental radiographs (X-ray photographs), prepare patients and equipment for dental procedures, and discharge office administrative functions under the supervision of dentists and dental hygienists. Includes instruction in medical record-keeping, general office duties, reception and patient intake, scheduling, equipment maintenance and sterilization, basic radiography, pre- and postoperative patient care and instruction, chairside assisting, and taking tooth and mouth impressions.

Dental Hygiene: A program that prepares individuals to clean teeth and apply preventive materials; provide oral health education and treatment counseling to patients; identify oral pathologies and injuries; and manage dental hygiene practices. Includes instruction in dental anatomy, microbiology, and pathology; dental hygiene theory and techniques; cleaning equipment operation and maintenance; dental materials; radiology; patient education and counseling; office management; supervised clinical training; and professional standards.

Dental Laboratory Technology: A program that prepares individuals, under the supervision of dentists, to design and construct dental prostheses such as caps, crowns, bridges, dentures, splints, and orthodontic appliances. Includes instruction in dental anatomy, dental materials, ceramics technology, impressions, complete dentures, partial dentures, orthodontics, crowns and bridges, sculpture, bonding and assembly techniques, and equipment operation.

Dietetics (RD): A program that prepares individuals to integrate and apply the principles of the food and nutrition sciences, human behavior, and the biomedical sciences to design and manage effective nutrition programs in a variety of settings. Includes instruction in human nutrition; nutrient metabolism; the role of foods and nutrition in health promotion and disease prevention; planning and directing food service activities; diet and nutrition analysis and planning; supervision of food storage and preparation; client education; and professional standards and regulations.

Emergency Medical Technology (EMT Paramedic): A program that prepares individuals, under the remote supervision of physicians, to recognize, assess, and manage medical emergencies in pre-hospital settings and to supervise ambulance personnel. Includes instruction in basic, intermediate, and advanced EMT procedures; emergency surgical procedures; medical triage; rescue operations; crisis scene management and personnel supervision; equipment operation and maintenance; patient stabilization, monitoring, and care; drug administration; identification and preliminary diagnosis of diseases and injuries; communication and computer operations; basic anatomy, physiology, pathology, and toxicology; and professional standards and regulations.

Health-Care Administration/Management: A program that prepares individuals to develop, plan, and manage health-care operations and services within health-care facilities and across health-care systems. Includes instruction in planning, business management, financial management, public relations, human resources management, health-care systems operation and management, health-care resource allocation and policy making, health law and regulations, and applications to specific types of health-care services.

Health Information/Medical Records Administration: A program that prepares individuals to plan, design, and manage systems, processes, and facilities used to collect, store, secure, retrieve, analyze, and transmit medical records and other health information used by clinical professionals and health-care organizations. Includes instruction in the principles and basic content of the biomedical and clinical sciences; information technology and applications; data and database management; clinical research methodologies; health information resources and systems; office management; legal requirements; and professional standards.

Health Services/Allied Health/Health Sciences: A general, introductory, undifferentiated, or joint program in health services occupations that prepares individuals for either entry into specialized training programs or for a variety of concentrations in the allied health area. Includes

instruction in the basic sciences, research and clinical procedures, and aspects of the subject matter related to various health occupations.

Hospital and Health-Care Facilities Administration/Management: A program that prepares individuals to apply managerial principles to the administration of hospitals, clinics, nursing homes, and other health-care facilities. Includes instruction in facilities planning, building and operations management, business management, financial management and insurance, fund-raising and marketing, public relations, human resources management and labor relations, health-care facilities operations, principles of health-care delivery, and applicable law and regulations.

Licensed Practical/Vocational Nurse Training (LPN, LVN): A program that prepares individuals to assist in providing general nursing care under the direction of a registered nurse, physician, or dentist. Includes instruction in taking patient vital signs, applying sterile dressings, educating patients, and assisting with examinations and treatment.

Medical/Clinical Assistant: A program that prepares individuals, under the supervision of physicians, to provide medical office administrative services and perform clinical duties, including patient intake and care, routine diagnostic and recording procedures, pre-examination and examination assistance, and the administration of medications and first aid. Includes instruction in basic anatomy and physiology; medical terminology; medical law and ethics; patient psychology and communications; medical office procedures; and clinical diagnostic, examination, testing, and treatment procedures.

Medical Office Management/Administration: A program that prepares individuals to manage the specialized business functions of a medical or clinical office. Includes instruction in business office operations, business and financial record-keeping, personnel supervision, medical and health-care policy administration, conference planning, scheduling and coordination, public relations, and applicable law and regulations.

Medical Transcription: A program that prepares individuals to execute verbatim medical conference minutes, medical reports, and medical orders. Includes instruction in dictation and simultaneous recording, analysis of notes and visual evidence, medical terminology, data processing applications and skills, formal medical report and correspondence formats, professional standards, and applicable law and regulations.

Nursing/Registered Nurse: A program that generally prepares individuals in the knowledge, techniques, and procedures for promoting health and providing care for sick, disabled, infirmed, or other individuals or groups. Includes instruction in administering medication and treatments, assisting a physician during treatments and examinations, referring patients to physicians and other health-care specialists, and planning education for health maintenance.

Pharmacy Technician/Assistant: A program that prepares individuals, under the supervision of pharmacists, to prepare medications; provide medications and related assistance to patients; and manage pharmacy, clinical, and business operations. Includes instruction in medical and pharmaceutical terminology, principles of pharmacology and pharmaceutics, drug identification, pharmacy laboratory procedures, prescription interpretation, patient communication and education, safety procedures, record-keeping, measurement and testing techniques, pharmacy business

operations, prescription preparation, logistics and dispensing operations, and applicable standards and regulations.

Physical Therapist Assistant: A program that prepares individuals, under the supervision of a physical therapist, to implement physical therapy treatment care plans, train patients, conduct treatment interventions, use equipment, and observe and record patient progress. Includes instruction in applied anatomy and physiology, applied kinesiology, principles and procedures of physical therapy, basic neurology and orthopedics, physical therapy modalities, documentation skills, psychosocial aspects of health care, wound and injury care, electrotherapy, working with orthotics and prostheses, and personal and professional ethics.

Physician Assistant: A program that prepares individuals to practice medicine, including diagnoses and treatment therapies, under the supervision of a physician. Includes instruction in the basic medical and clinical sciences and specialized preparation in fields such as family medicine; pediatrics; obstetrics; gynecology; general surgery; psychiatry; behavioral medicine; the delivery of health-care services to homebound patients, rural populations, underserved populations; and community health services.

Pre-Medicine: A program that prepares individuals for the independent, professional practice of medicine, involving the prevention, diagnosis, and treatment of illnesses, injuries, and other disorders of the human body. Includes instruction in the basic medical sciences; clinical medicine; examination and diagnosis; patient communications; medical ethics and law; and professional standards and rotations in specialties such as internal medicine, surgery, pediatrics, obstetrics and gynecology, orthopedics, neurology, ophthalmology, radiology, clinical pathology, anesthesiology, family medicine, and psychiatry.

Public Health: A program that generally prepares individuals to plan, manage, and evaluate public health-care services and to function as public health officers. Includes instruction in epidemiology, biostatistics, public health principles, preventive medicine, health policy and regulations, health-care services and related administrative functions, public health law enforcement, health economics and budgeting, public communications, and professional standards and ethics.

Radiation Protection/Health Physics Technician: A program that prepares individuals, under the supervision of health physicists, occupational safety and health specialists, and public health officials, to monitor and control radiation exposure and implement preventive measures in health-care, work, and natural environments. Includes instruction in radiation physics, environmental radioactivity, radiological instrumentation, electronics of radiation detection equipment, radioactive waste management and control, safety and handling procedures, decontamination procedures, radioactivity testing and analysis, and communications skills.

Speech-Language Pathology: A program that prepares individuals to evaluate the speaking, language interpretation, and related physiological and cognitive capabilities of children and/or adults and develop treatment and rehabilitative solutions in consultation with clinicians and educators. Includes instruction in the anatomy and physiology of speech and hearing, biomechanics of swallowing and vocal articulation, communications disorders, psychology of auditory function and cognitive communication, language assessment and diagnostic techniques, and rehabilitative and management therapies.

Veterinary/Animal Health Technology and Veterinary Assistant: A program that prepares individuals, under the supervision of veterinarians, laboratory animal specialists, and zoological professionals, to provide patient management, care, and clinical procedures assistance as well as owner communication. Includes instruction in animal nursing care, animal health and nutrition, animal handling, clinical pathology, radiology, anesthesiology, dental prophylaxis, surgical assisting, clinical laboratory procedures, office administration skills, patient and owner management, and applicable standards and regulations.

Hospitality, Tourism, and Recreation

This career cluster includes majors that appeal to students with an interest in providing others with a clean environment, good food and drink, comfortable accommodations, and recreation.

Adult Development and Aging: A program that focuses on the characteristics of aging populations and the needs of older individuals in family and institutional settings. Includes instruction in the biological and psychological stages of aging; the provision of dependent care; serving the social, economic, and psychological needs of aging adults; related public policy issues; and adult community resources.

Aesthetician/Esthetician and Skin Care Specialist: A program that prepares individuals to cleanse, depilate, massage, and beautify the human body and to function as licensed estheticians and skin care specialists. Includes instruction in skin anatomy, physiology, and health; principles of nutrition; decontamination and infection control; health and safety; facial and body massage; body wrapping and spa treatments; temporary hair removal including waxing and tweezing; color and skin analysis; client consultation and care; applicable laws and regulations; business practices; and sometimes related alternative healing regimens.

Apparel and Textiles: A general program that focuses on the development of textile products and their distribution and use in terms of the psychological, social, economic, and physical needs of consumers. Includes instruction in the production, distribution, marketing, and end use of various apparel and textile products.

Baking and Pastry Arts/Baker/Pastry Chef: A program that prepares individuals to serve as professional bakers and pastry specialists in restaurants or other commercial baking establishments. Includes instruction in bread and pastry making, bread and pastry handling and storage, cake and pastry decorating, baking industry operations, product packaging and marketing operations, and counter display and service.

Barbering: A program that prepares individuals to shave and trim facial/neck hair and beards, cut and dress hair, fit hairpieces, give facial and scalp massages, apply cosmetic treatments, and to prepare for licensure as professional barbers at various levels. Includes instruction in facial shaving, beard and mustache shaping and trimming, shampooing, hair cutting, hair styles and styling art, facial treatments and massage, chemical applications, hair and scalp anatomy and physiology, hairpiece and toupee fitting, equipment operation, health and safety, customer service, and shop business practices.

Child Development: A program that focuses on the intellectual, social, emotional, and biological development of children and the planning and design of related human services. Includes instruction in parent-child relations, parenting practices, special needs of children, parental and environmental influences on child development, external support services, and related public policy issues.

Consumer Economics: A program that focuses on the application of micro- and macroeconomic theory to consumer behavior and individual and family consumption of goods and services. Includes instruction in modeling, economic forecasting, indexing, price theory, and analysis of individual commodities and services and/or groups of related commodities and services.

Cooking and Related Culinary Arts: A program that focuses on the general study of the cooking and related culinary arts and that may prepare individuals for a variety of jobs within the food service industry. Includes instruction in food preparation, cooking techniques, equipment operation and maintenance, sanitation and safety, communication skills, applicable regulations, and principles of food service management.

Cosmetology: A program that generally prepares individuals to cut, trim, and style scalp, facial, and body hair; apply cosmetic preparations; perform manicures and pedicures; massage the head and extremities; and prepare for practice as licensed cosmetologists in specialized or full-service salons. Includes instruction in hair cutting and styling, manicuring, pedicuring, facial treatments, shampooing, chemical applications, esthetics, shop management, sanitation and safety, customer service, and applicable professional and labor laws and regulations.

Facilities Planning and Management: A program that focuses on strategic workplace and facility planning and that prepares individuals to function as facility and event managers and workplace consultants. Includes instruction in the principles of aesthetic and functional design, environmental psychology and organizational behavior, real estate planning, principles of occupational health and safety, event planning and management, operations management, and applicable regulatory and policy issues.

Family and Consumer Sciences/Human Sciences: A general program that focuses on family and consumer sciences, including how individuals develop and function in family, work, and community settings and how they relate to their physical, social, emotional, and intellectual environments.

Food Service Systems Administration/Management: A program that focuses on the principles and practices relating to the administration of food service systems in institutional settings and that prepares individuals to manage such operations in public and private facilities. Includes instruction in human nutrition, food safety, the design and organization of food service systems, purchasing, personnel management, and related business practices.

Funeral Direction/Service: A program that prepares individuals for professional licensure as funeral directors and as managers of funeral homes, cemeteries, and related services. Includes instruction in the sociology of death and dying, psychology of grief and grief counseling, history of funeral service, funeral direction, business law, funeral service law, funeral home management, accounting and related computer operations, and funeral services marketing and merchandising.

Health and Physical Education: A general program that focuses on activities and principles that promote physical fitness, achieve and maintain athletic prowess, and accomplish related research and service goals. Includes instruction in human movement studies, motivation studies, rules and practice of specific sports, exercise and fitness principles and techniques, basic athletic injury prevention and treatment, and organizing and leading fitness and sports programs.

Human Development and Family Studies: A general program that focuses on basic human developmental and behavioral characteristics of the individual within the context of the family. Includes instruction in the conditions that influence human growth and development, strategies that promote growth and development across the life span, and the study of family systems.

Human Nutrition: A program that focuses on the relationships between food consumption and human development and health. Includes instruction in the cellular and molecular processes of food processing in the human body, related metabolic processes, the relationship of food and nutrition to disease, and nutritional needs across the life span.

Kinesiology and Exercise Science: A scientific program that focuses on the anatomy, physiology, biochemistry, and biophysics of human movement and applications to exercise and therapeutic rehabilitation. Includes instruction in biomechanics, motor behavior, motor development and coordination, motor neurophysiology, performance research, rehabilitative therapies, the development of diagnostic and rehabilitative methods and equipment, and related analytical methods and procedures in applied exercise and therapeutic rehabilitation.

Mortuary Science and Embalming: A program that prepares individuals for licensure as embalmers and morticians. Includes instruction in pathogenic microbiology, systematic pathology, thanatochemistry, gross anatomy, clinical mortuary science, embalming, restorative art, applicable laws and regulations, and special services such as cremation and preparations required by specific religious communities.

Parks, Recreation, and Leisure Studies: A program that focuses on the principles underlying recreational and leisure activities, and the practices involved in providing indoor and outdoor recreational facilities and services for the general public.

Restaurant, Culinary, and Catering Management: A program that prepares individuals to plan, supervise, and manage food and beverage preparation and service operations, restaurant facilities, and catering services. Includes instruction in food/beverage industry operations, cost control, purchasing and storage, business administration, logistics, personnel management, culinary arts, restaurant and menu planning, executive chef functions, event planning and management, health and safety, insurance, and applicable law and regulations.

Sport and Fitness Administration/Management: A program that prepares individuals to apply business, coaching, and physical education principles to the organization, administration and management of athletic programs and teams, fitness/rehabilitation facilities and health clubs, sport recreation services, and related services. Includes instruction in program planning and development; business and financial management principles; sales, marketing, and recruitment; event promotion, scheduling, and management; facilities management; public relations; legal aspects of sports; and applicable health and safety standards.

Textile Science: A program that focuses on the properties and processing of fibers, yarns, whole fabrics, dyes, and finishes, both natural and synthetic. Includes instruction in the chemical and physical properties of textile materials, end-use analysis, interior furnishing applications, and industrial applications.

Therapeutic Recreation/Recreational Therapy: A program that prepares individuals to plan, organize, and direct recreational activities designed to promote health and well-being for patients who are physically, mentally, or emotionally disabled. Includes instruction in the foundations of therapeutic recreation, leisure education and counseling, program planning, therapeutic recreational modalities, basic anatomy and physiology, psychology, medical terminology, human growth and development, patient observation and evaluation, special needs populations, and professional standards and ethics.

Tourism and Travel Services Management: A program that prepares individuals to manage travel-related enterprises and related convention and/or tour services. Includes instruction in travel agency management, tour arranging and planning, convention and event planning, travel industry operations and procedures, tourism marketing and promotion strategies, travel counseling, travel industry law, international and domestic operations, and travel and tourism policy.

Human Service

This career cluster includes majors that appeal to students with an interest in improving people's social, mental, emotional, or spiritual well-being.

Art Therapy: A program that prepares individuals, in consultation with other rehabilitation team members or in private practice, to use drawing and other art media forms to assess, treat, and rehabilitate individuals with mental, emotional, developmental, or physical disorders. Includes instruction in art, history and theory of art therapy, art therapeutic techniques, psychopathology, patient assessment and diagnosis, cultural diversity issues, legal and ethical practice issues, and professional standards and regulations.

Clinical Child Psychology: A program that focuses on the developmental processes of children and associated disorders and that prepares individuals for the independent professional practice of clinical child psychology. Includes instruction in developmental neuropsychology, child psychopathology, testing of children and adolescents, pediatric psychology, psychosocial variables in child development, clinical skills, family therapy, behavioral assessment and intervention, clinical skills, consultation, professional standards and ethics, and applications to topics such as infancy, childhood, and adolescence.

Clinical/Medical Social Work: A program that prepares individuals for the specialized professional practice of social work, in collaboration with other health-care professionals, in hospitals and other health-care facilities and organizations. Includes instruction in social work, psychiatric case work, clinical interviewing techniques, therapeutic intervention strategies, patient testing and evaluation, patient and family counseling, social rehabilitation, patient care planning, recordkeeping, and support services liaison.

Clinical Pastoral Counseling/Patient Counseling: A program that prepares ordained clergy and other counseling professionals to respond to the emotional and spiritual needs of patients and families in health-care emergencies and other situations, and to consult with and counsel other health-care professionals. Includes instruction in advanced interpersonal communication; individual and small group counseling; interdisciplinary teamwork; crisis management; extended-care relationships; self-analysis; medical ethics; pastoral care art; spiritual dimensions of human growth and health; counseling psychology and therapy; and applications to grief, death, emotional collapse, injury, individual/family adjustment, and chronic illness situations.

Clinical Psychology: A program that prepares individuals for the independent, professional practice of clinical psychology, involving the analysis, diagnosis, and clinical treatment of psychological disorders and behavioral pathologies. Includes instruction in clinical assessment and diagnosis, personality appraisal, psychopathology, clinical psychopharmacology, behavior modification, therapeutic intervention skills, patient interviewing, personalized and group therapy, child and adolescent therapy, cognitive and behavioral therapy, supervised clinical practice, ethical standards, and applicable regulations.

Cognitive Psychology and Psycholinguistics: A program that focuses on the scientific study of the mechanisms and processes of learning and thinking and associated information-encoding, decoding, processing, and transmitting systems. Includes instruction in theories of cognition and intelligence; studies of cognitive processes such as memory, sensation, perception, pattern recognition, problem solving, and conceptual thinking; cybernetics; psycholinguistics; and the study of biological and social communications mechanisms and processes.

Community Health Services/Liaison/Counseling: A program that prepares individuals to serve as facilitators, advocates, and referral professionals linking health care and related social services with affected recipient communities. Includes instruction in public and community health, human and social services, health services administration, group counseling, health education, group advocacy, cross-cultural and multilingual communication, and applicable laws and policies.

Community Psychology: A program that prepares individuals to apply psychological principles to the analysis of social problems and the implementation of intervention strategies for addressing these problems. Includes instruction in social ecology, primary and secondary prevention of social pathologies, social intervention strategies and tactics, large-group counseling, social services systems behavior, creating settings, cultural stress, and the dynamics of social change.

Comparative Psychology: A program that focuses on the behavior of members of particular species or groups and the relationship of the behaviors of the species or group to their evolutionary origins. Includes instruction in differential psychology, experimental and physiological psychology, psychopharmacology, psychology of individual differences, reinforcement theory, and neurophysiology.

Counseling Psychology: A program that prepares individuals for the independent professional practice of psychological counseling, involving the rendering of therapeutic services to individuals and groups experiencing psychological problems and exhibiting distress symptoms. Includes instruction in counseling theory, therapeutic intervention strategies, patient/counselor relationships, testing and assessment methods and procedures, group therapy, marital and family therapy,

child and adolescent therapy, supervised counseling practice, ethical standards, and applicable regulations.

Dance Therapy: A program that prepares individuals, in consultation with other rehabilitation team members or in private practice, to use the therapeutic application of creative dance movement to assist in promoting client rehabilitation and physical, emotional, and mental health. Includes instruction in neuroanatomy, personality development, movement and motor behavior, psychology, dance, creative expression modalities, improvisation, group psychology and leadership, client evaluation and supervision, dance therapy practice, and professional standards and ethics.

Developmental and Child Psychology: A program that focuses on the scientific study of the psychological growth and development of individuals from infancy through adulthood. Includes instruction in cognitive and perceptual development, emotional development, personality development, the effects of biological maturation on behavior, theories of cognitive growth and related research methods, testing and assessment methods for different age levels, research on child and adolescent behavior therapy, and the psychology of aging.

Educational Psychology: A program that focuses on the application of psychology to the study of the behavior of individuals in the roles of teacher and learner; the nature and effects of learning environments; and the psychological effects of methods, resources, organization and nonschool experience on the educational process. Includes instruction in learning theory, human growth and development, research methods, and psychological evaluation.

Environmental Psychology: A program that focuses on the study of behavioral interactions between human beings and the environment in individual and group contexts, and ways to improve them. Includes instruction in contextual theory; statistics; physiological, social, and psychological responses to natural and technological hazards and disease; environmental perception and cognition; loneliness and stress; and psychological aspects of environmental design and planning.

Experimental Psychology: A program that focuses on the scientific study of behavior under experimental conditions and the analysis of controlled behavioral responses. Includes instruction in learning theory, research design and experimental methods, psychological measurement, statistical design and methods, analysis of cognitive and behavioral variables, and the conduct of specialized and large-scale studies.

Family Psychology: A program that prepares individuals to provide therapeutic, evaluative, and research services to families and individuals in the family unit context. Includes instruction in natural and family systems theory, family and group rituals, family evaluation and assessment, marital and couples therapy, sex therapy, parenting, interviewing techniques, genogram construction, family sculpting, diversity issues, family violence, family law, and professional standards and ethics.

Genetic Counseling: A program that prepares individuals to counsel patients and families concerning inherited genetic disorders and diseases and children with birth defects, assess risk factors and planning options associated with potential and actual inherited conditions, and serve as patient advocates and provide referral services in relation to private and public support services. Includes instruction in clinical/medical genetics, methods of genetic testing, interviewing and counseling skills, genetic and support services delivery, principles of public health, medical ethics, law and regulations, patient advocacy, and professional standards.

Geropsychology: A program that focuses on the psychology of aging and of elderly individuals and populations, with reference to growth and decline across the life span. Includes instruction in gerontology, developmental and adult psychology, age-related development and decline of cognitive processes, age-related psychological and neurological disorders, social and personality development in aging populations and individuals, and applications to the clinical treatment and care of older adults.

Industrial and Organizational Psychology: A program that focuses on the scientific study of individual and group behavior in institutional settings, applications to related problems of organization and industry, and that may prepare individuals to apply such principles in industrial and organizational settings. Includes instruction in group behavior theory, organizational theory, reward/punishment structures, human-machine and human-computer interactions, motivation dynamics, human stress studies, environmental and organizational influences on behavior, alienation and satisfaction, and job testing and assessment.

Marriage and Family Therapy/Counseling: A program that prepares individuals for the independent professional practice of marriage and family therapy, involving the diagnosis of cognitive, affective, and behavioral domain disorders, both mental and emotional, within the context of marriage and family systems and the application of short- and long-term therapeutic strategies in family group contexts. Includes instruction in psychotherapy, family systems and studies, small group intervention and therapy, marital problems, depression, identification of psychopathologies and behavioral disorders, holistic health care, practice management, applicable regulations, and professional standards and ethics.

Mental Health Counseling: A program that prepares individuals to provide evaluations, referrals, and short-term counseling services to help people prevent or remediate personal problems, conflicts, and emotional crises. Includes instruction in human development, psychopathology, individual and group counseling, personality theory, career assessment, patient screening and referral, observation and testing techniques, interviewing skills, professional standards and ethics, and applicable laws and regulations.

Movement Therapy and Movement Education: A program that prepares individuals to use functional and expressive integration strategies to help promote somatic awareness and optimal psychophysical functioning. Includes instruction in skilled touch techniques, kinesthetic awareness processes, movement observation, patterning, client assessment and guidance, verbal and nonverbal communication, practice management, professional standards and ethics, and specific therapeutic and educational modalities (Alexander Technique, Aston Patterning, Body-Mind Centering, Feldenkrais Method, Laban Movement Analysis, Trager Approach, and others).

Music Therapy: A program that prepares individuals, in association with a rehabilitation team or in private practice, to use music in therapeutic relationships to address patients' physical, psychological, cognitive, emotional, and social needs. Includes instruction in music theory and performance, human growth and development, biomedical sciences, abnormal psychology, disabling conditions, patient assessment and diagnosis, treatment plan development and implementation, clinical evaluation, record-keeping, and professional standards and ethics.

Psychiatric/Mental Health Services Technician: A program that prepares individuals, under the supervision of psychiatrists, psychologists, nurses, and other mental health-care professionals, to provide direct patient care services, assist in developing and implementing treatment plans, administer medications, and perform related administrative functions. Includes instruction in mental health theory, applied psychopathology, patient communication and management, crisis intervention, psychotropic medication, mental health treatment procedures, substance abuse, record-keeping, clinical administrative skills, and applicable standards and regulations.

Psychoanalysis and Psychotherapy: A program that prepares individuals to practice the provision of psychoanalytic counseling to individuals and groups based on the psychodynamic principles evolved from authorities such as Freud, Adler, and Jung. Includes instruction in self-analysis, personality theory, dream analysis, free association and transference theory and techniques, psychodynamic theory, developmental processes, applications to specific clinical conditions, practice management, and professional standards and ethics.

Psychology: A general program that focuses on the scientific study of individual and collective behavior, the physical and environmental bases of behavior, and the analysis and treatment of behavior problems and disorders. Includes instruction in the principles of the various subfields of psychology, research methods, and psychological assessment and testing methods.

School Psychology: A program that prepares individuals to apply clinical and counseling psychology principles to the diagnosis and treatment of student behavioral problems. Includes instruction in child and/or adolescent development; learning theory; testing, observation and other procedures for assessing educational, personality, intelligence and motor skill development; therapeutic intervention strategies for students and families; identification and classification of disabilities and disorders affecting learning; school psychological services planning; supervised counseling practice; ethical standards; and applicable regulations.

Social Psychology: A program that focuses on the scientific study of individual behavior in group contexts, group behavior, and associated phenomena. Includes instruction in social learning theory, group theory and dynamics, sex roles, social cognition and inference, attribution theory, attitude formation, criminal behavior and other social pathologies, altruistic behavior, social development, and social ecology.

Substance Abuse/Addiction Counseling: A program that prepares individuals to help prevent substance abuse, counsel individuals and families with drug and alcohol problems, and perform intervention and therapeutic services for persons suffering from addiction. Includes instruction in individual and group counseling skills, psychology of addiction, sociology, crisis intervention, substance abuse identification methodologies, substance abuse treatment modalities, substance abuse prevention and treatment resources, pharmacology and behavioral aspects of abused substances, treatment evaluation, patient observation and education, group dynamics, professional standards and ethics, and applicable law and regulations.

Vocational Rehabilitation Counseling: A program that prepares individuals to counsel disabled individuals and recovering patients in psychological, personal, social, and vocational adjustment in order to have fulfilling and productive lives. Includes instruction in patient evaluation and testing, rehabilitation program planning, patient support services and referral, job analysis, adjustment

psychology, rehabilitation services provision, patient counseling and education, applicable law and regulations, and professional standards and ethics.

Information Technology

This career cluster includes majors that appeal to students with an interest in designing, developing, managing, and supporting information systems.

Artificial Intelligence and Robotics: A program that focuses on the symbolic inference, representation, and simulation by computers and software of human learning and reasoning processes and capabilities, and the modeling of human motor control and motions by computer-driven machinery. Includes instruction in computing theory; cybernetics; human factors; natural language processing; robot design; and applicable aspects of engineering, technology, and specific end-use applications.

Computer Graphics: A program that focuses on the software, hardware, and mathematical tools used to represent, display, and manipulate topological, two-, and three-dimensional objects on a computer screen and that prepares individuals to function as computer graphics specialists. Includes instruction in graphics software and systems; digital multimedia; graphic design; graphics devices, processors, and standards; attributes and transformations; projections; surface identification and rendering; color theory and application; and applicable geometry and algorithms.

Computer and Information Systems Security: A program that prepares individuals to assess the security needs of computer and network systems, recommend safeguard solutions, and manage the implementation and maintenance of security devices, systems, and procedures. Includes instruction in computer architecture, programming, and systems analysis; networking; telecommunications; cryptography; security system design; applicable law and regulations; risk assessment and policy analysis; contingency planning; user access issues; investigation techniques; and troubleshooting.

Computer Programming: A program that focuses on the general writing and implementation of generic and customized programs to drive operating systems and that generally prepares individuals to apply the methods and procedures of software design and programming to software installation and maintenance. Includes instruction in software design, low- and high-level languages and program writing, program customization and linking, prototype testing, troubleshooting, and related aspects of operating systems and networks.

Computer Science: A general program that focuses on computers, computing problems and solutions, and the design of computer systems and user interfaces from a scientific perspective. Includes instruction in the principles of computational science and computing theory, computer hardware design, computer development and programming, and applications to a variety of end-use situations.

Computer Support Specialist: A program that prepares individuals to provide technical assistance, support, and advice to computer users to help troubleshoot software and hardware problems. Includes instruction in computer concepts, information systems, networking, operating systems, computer hardware, the Internet, software applications, help desk concepts and problem solving, and principles of customer service.

Computer Systems Analysis: A program that prepares individuals to apply programming and systems analysis principles to the selection, implementation, and troubleshooting of customized computer and software installations across the life cycle. Includes instruction in computer hardware and software; compilation, composition, execution, and operating systems; low- and high-level languages and language programming; programming and debugging techniques; installation and maintenance testing and documentation; process and data flow analysis; user needs analysis and documentation; cost-benefit analysis; and specification design.

Computer Systems Networking and Telecommunications: A program that focuses on the design, implementation, and management of linked systems of computers, peripherals, and associated software to maximize efficiency and productivity and that prepares individuals to function as network specialists and managers at various levels. Includes instruction in operating systems and applications, systems design and analysis, networking theory and solutions, types of networks, network management and control, network and flow optimization, security, configuring, and troubleshooting.

Data Modeling/Warehousing and Database Administration: A program that prepares individuals to design and manage the construction of databases and related software programs and applications, including the linking of individual data sets to create complex searchable databases (warehousing) and the use of analytical search tools (mining). Includes instruction in database theory, logic, and semantics; operational and warehouse modeling; dimensionality; attributes and hierarchies; data definition; technical architecture; access and security design; integration; formatting and extraction; data delivery; index design; implementation problems; planning and budgeting; and client and networking issues.

Data Processing and Data Processing Technology: A program that prepares individuals to master and use computer software programs and applications for inputting, verifying, organizing, storing, retrieving, transforming (changing, updating, and deleting), and extracting information. Includes instruction in using various operating system configurations and in types of data entry such as word processing, spreadsheets, calculators, management programs, design programs, database programs, and research programs.

Information Science/Studies: A program that focuses on the theory, organization, and process of information collection, transmission, and utilization in traditional and electronic forms. Includes instruction in information classification and organization; information storage and processing; transmission, transfer, and signaling; communications and networking; systems planning and design; human interfacing and use analysis; database development; information policy analysis; and related aspects of hardware, software, economics, social factors, and capacity.

Information Technology: A program that focuses on the design of technological information systems, including computing systems, as solutions to business and research data and communications support needs. Includes instruction in the principles of computer hardware and software components, algorithms, databases, telecommunications, user tactics, application testing, and human interface design.

System Administration: A program that prepares individuals to manage the computer operations and control the system configurations emanating from a specific site or network hub. Includes

instruction in computer hardware and software and applications, local area (LAN) and wide area (WAN) networking, principles of information systems security, disk space and traffic load monitoring, data backup, resource allocation, and setup and takedown procedures.

System, Networking, and LAN/WAN Management: A program that prepares individuals to oversee and regulate the computer system and performance requirements of an entire organization or network of satellite users. Includes instruction in performance balancing, redundancy, local area network (LAN) and wide area network (WAN) management, system migration and upgrading, outage control, problem diagnosis and troubleshooting, and system maintenance budgeting and management.

Web/Multimedia Management and Webmaster: A program that prepares individuals to develop and maintain web servers and the hosted web pages at one or a group of websites, and to function as designated webmasters. Includes instruction in computer systems and networks, server installation and maintenance, web page design and editing, information resources management, web policy and procedures, Internet applications of information systems security, user interfacing and usability research, and relevant management and communications skills.

Web Page, Digital/Multimedia, and Information Resources Design: A program that prepares individuals to apply HTML, XML, JavaScript, graphics applications, and other authoring tools to the design, editing, and publishing (launching) of documents, images, graphics, sound, and multimedia products on the World Wide Web. Includes instruction in Internet theory, web page standards and policies, elements of web page design, user interfaces, vector tools, special effects, interactive and multimedia components, search engines, navigation, morphing, e-commerce tools, and emerging web technologies.

Law and Public Safety

This career cluster includes majors that appeal to students with an interest in upholding people's rights or in protecting people and property.

Corrections: A program that prepares individuals to study the theories and principles of correctional science and to function as professional corrections officers and other workers in public and/or private incarceration facilities.

Court Reporting: A program that prepares individuals to record and transcribe examinations, testimony, judicial orders and instructions, legal opinions, and other formal proceedings via print or electronic methods. Includes instruction in legal terminology, legal transcription, shorthand, verbatim recording, equipment operation and procedures, applicable regulations, and professional standards and ethics.

Criminal Justice/Police Science: A program that prepares individuals to perform the duties of police and public security officers, including patrol and investigative activities, traffic control, crowd control and public relations, witness interviewing, evidence collection and management, basic crime prevention methods, weapon and equipment operation and maintenance, report preparation and other routine law enforcement responsibilities.

Criminal Justice/Safety Studies: A program that focuses on the criminal justice system, its organizational components and processes, and its legal and public policy contexts. Includes instruction in criminal law and policy, police and correctional systems organization, the administration of justice and the judiciary, and public attitudes regarding criminal justice issues.

Criminalistics and Criminal Science: A program that focuses on the application of clinical and criminal laboratory science, investigative techniques, and criminology to the reconstruction of crimes and the analysis of physical evidence. Includes instruction in laboratory science, laboratory procedures, criminology and police science, evidentiary testing and analysis, computer applications, record-keeping, reconstruction techniques, evidence handling and storage, and applications to specific types of evidence and crimes.

Fire Protection and Safety Technology: A program that prepares individuals to apply a knowledge of fire prevention and control skills to problems of reducing fire risk, loss limitation, supervising substance removal, conducting fire investigations, and advising on matters of safety procedures and fire prevention policy.

Fire Science/Firefighting: A program that prepares individuals to perform the duties of fire fighters. Includes instruction in firefighting equipment operation and maintenance, principles of fire science and combustible substances, methods of controlling different types of fires, hazardous material handling and control, fire rescue procedures, public relations, and applicable laws and regulations.

Forensic Psychology: A program that prepares individuals to apply clinical, counseling, school, and neuropsychology skills to the provision of psychological services within the criminal justice and civil legal systems, including consultation, assessment, and interventions. Includes instruction in the epidemiology of mental/behavioral disorders, risk factors for violence and criminality, profiling and patterning, psychological testing, prediction and intervention measurement, forensic assessment, criminal and civil law and procedures, secure environments, forensic treatment and intervention skills, and professional standards and ethics.

Forensic Science and Technology: A program that focuses on the application of the physical, biomedical, and social sciences to the analysis and evaluation of physical evidence, human testimony, and criminal suspects. Includes instruction in forensic medicine, forensic dentistry, anthropology, psychology, pathology, forensic laboratory technology, crime scene analysis, fingerprint technology, document analysis, pattern analysis, examination procedures, applicable law and regulations, and professional standards and ethics.

Juvenile Corrections: A program that prepares individuals to specialize in the provision of correction services to underage minor populations. Includes instruction in corrections, juvenile delinquency, juvenile development and psychology, juvenile law, justice administration, social services, record-keeping procedures, and communication skills.

Law: A program that prepares individuals for the independent, professional practice of law; for taking state and national bar examinations; and for advanced research in jurisprudence. Includes instruction in the theory and practice of the legal system, including the statutory, administrative, and judicial components of civil and criminal law.

Legal Assistant/Paralegal: A program that prepares individuals to perform research, drafting, investigatory, record-keeping, and related administrative functions under the supervision of an attorney or court. Includes instruction in legal research, drafting legal documents, appraising, pleading, courthouse procedures, and legal specializations.

Pre-Law Studies: A program that prepares individuals for the professional study of law at the post-baccalaureate level.

Security and Loss Prevention Services: A program that prepares individuals to perform routine inspection, patrol, and crime prevention services for private clients. Includes instruction in the provision of personal protection as well as property security.

Manufacturing

This career cluster includes majors that appeal to students with an interest in processing materials into products or maintaining and repairing products by using machines or hand tools.

Appliance Installation and Repair Technology: A program that prepares individuals to apply technical knowledge and skills to repair, install, and service major gas, electric, and microwave consumer appliances such as stoves, refrigerators, dryers, water heaters, washers, dishwashers, and commercial units such as ice makers and coffee makers.

Communications Systems Installation and Repair Technology: A program that prepares individuals to apply technical knowledge and skills to assemble, install, operate, maintain, and repair one- and two- way communications equipment and systems, including television cable systems and mobile or stationary communication devices. Includes instruction in diagnostic techniques; the use of testing equipment; and the principles of mechanics, electricity, and electronics as they relate to the repair of communications systems.

Computer Installation and Repair Technology: A program that prepares individuals to apply technical knowledge and skills to assemble, install, operate, maintain, and repair computers and related instruments. Includes instruction in power supplies, number systems, memory structure, buffers and registers, microprocessor design, peripheral equipment, programming, and networking.

Electrical/Electronics Equipment Installation and Repair: A program that generally prepares individuals to apply technical knowledge and skills to operate, maintain, and repair electrical and electronic equipment. Includes instruction in electrical circuitry, simple gearing, linkages and lubrication of machines and appliances, and the use of testing equipment.

Furniture Design and Manufacturing: A program that prepares individuals to apply technical knowledge and skills to prepare and execute furniture design projects, assemble and finish furniture articles or subassemblies, repair furniture, and use a variety of hand and power tools.

Heating, Air Conditioning, Ventilation, and Refrigeration Maintenance Technology (HAC, HACR, HVAC, HVACR): A program that prepares individuals to apply technical knowledge and skills to repair, install, service, and maintain the operating condition of heating, air conditioning,

and refrigeration systems. Includes instruction in diagnostic techniques; the use of testing equipment; and the principles of mechanics, electricity, and electronics as they relate to the repair of heating, air conditioning, and refrigeration systems.

Industrial Electronics Technology: A program that prepares individuals to apply technical knowledge and skills to assemble, install, operate, maintain, and repair electrical/electronic equipment used in industry and manufacturing. Includes instruction in installing, maintaining, and testing various types of equipment.

Ironworking/Ironworker: A program that prepares individuals to make and install structural, ornamental, and reinforcing metal structures and supports. Includes instruction in drafting, technical mathematics, blueprint interpretation, welding, riveting, beam placement, ornamental design, structural reinforcement, crane operation, safety, and applicable codes and standards.

Machine Tool Technology/Machinist: A program that prepares individuals to apply technical knowledge and skills to plan, manufacture, assemble, test, and repair parts, mechanisms, machines, and structures in which materials are cast, formed, shaped, molded, heat treated, cut, twisted, pressed, fused, stamped, or worked.

Security System Installation, Repair, and Inspection Technology: A program that prepares individuals to apply technical knowledge and skills to install and repair household, business, and industrial security alarms, sensors, video and sound recording devices, identification systems, protective barriers, and related technologies.

Sheet Metal Technology/Sheetworking: A program that prepares individuals to apply technical knowledge and skills to form, shape, bend, and fold extruded metals, including the creation of new products, using hand tools and machines such as cornice brakes, forming rolls, and squaring shears.

Tool and Die Technology: A program that prepares individuals to apply technical knowledge and skills to operate machine tools used in the forming of metal components, as well as the fabrication of special tools, dies, jigs, and fixtures used in cutting, working, and finishing metal components.

Welding Technology/Welder: A program that prepares individuals to apply technical knowledge and skills to join or cut metal surfaces. Includes instruction in arc welding, resistance welding, brazing and soldering, cutting, high-energy beam welding and cutting, solid state welding, ferrous and nonferrous materials, oxidation-reduction reactions, welding metallurgy, welding processes and heat treating, structural design, safety, and applicable codes and standards.

Retail and Wholesale Sales and Service

This career cluster includes majors that appeal to students with an interest in bringing others to a particular point of view through personal persuasion and sales techniques.

Auctioneering: A program that prepares individuals for professional careers as auctioneers and auction managers and for meeting applicable state licensing requirements. Includes instruction in bid calling; public speaking; ringworking; auction techniques; salesmanship skills; auction

clerking and cashiering; auction advertising; working independently or with auction houses; contracts and agency; applicable sales law; and managing both general auctions and auctions specializing in commodities such as antiques, consignments, farm equipment, industrial equipment, real estate, livestock, and automobiles.

Fashion Merchandising: A program that prepares individuals to promote product lines/brands and organize promotional campaigns at the wholesale level to attract retailer interest, wholesale purchasing, and supply contracts. Includes instruction in wholesaling, wholesale advertising, selling, and customer relations.

Fashion Modeling: A program that prepares individuals to present and display fashion, apparel, and accessories products in wholesale and retail settings, either on the person or via props and natural or artificial settings. Includes instruction in modeling skills, health and cosmetic principles, fashion show management, display design and production, and applicable aspects of advertising and fashion photography.

International Marketing: A program that prepares individuals to perform marketing activities in enterprises primarily engaged in exporting or importing goods and services in world markets. Includes instruction in international trade controls, foreign trade operations, locating markets, negotiation practices, monetary issues, and international public relations.

Marketing/Marketing Management: A program that generally prepares individuals to undertake and manage the process of developing consumer audiences and moving products from producers to consumers. Includes instruction in buyer behavior and dynamics, principles of marketing research, demand analysis, cost-volume and profit relationships, pricing theory, marketing campaign and strategic planning, market segments, advertising methods, sales operations and management, consumer relations, retailing, and applications to specific products and markets.

Marketing Research: A program that prepares individuals to provide analytical descriptions of consumer behavior patterns and market environments to marketing managers and other business decision makers. Includes instruction in survey research methods, research design, new product test marketing, exploratory marketing, consumer needs and preferences analysis, geographic analysis, and applications to specific products and markets.

Merchandising and Buying Operations: A program that prepares individuals to function as professional buyers of resale products and product lines for stores, chains, and other retail enterprises. Includes instruction in product evaluation, merchandising, applicable aspects of brand and consumer research, principles of purchasing, and negotiation skills.

Retailing and Retail Operations: A program that prepares individuals to perform operations associated with retail sales in a variety of settings. Includes instruction in over-the-counter and other direct sales operations in business settings, basic bookkeeping principles, customer service, team/ staff leadership and supervision, floor management, and applicable technical skills.

Sales, Distribution, and Marketing Operations: A program that focuses on the general process and techniques of direct wholesale and retail buying and selling operations and introduces individuals to related careers. Includes instruction in the principles of entrepreneurial economics, basic

sales skills, the distribution channels for goods and services, and supervised practical application experiences.

Selling Skills and Sales Operations: A program that prepares individuals to possess the skills associated with direct promotion of products and services to potential customers and to function as independent sales representatives and managers. Includes instruction in consumer psychology, image projection, public speaking and interpersonal communications, sales organization and operations, customer relations, professional standards and ethics, and applicable technical skills.

Scientific Research, Engineering, and Mathematics

This career cluster includes majors that appeal to students with an interest in discovering, collecting, and analyzing information about the natural world, life sciences, and human behavior.

Anthropology: A program that focuses on the systematic study of human beings, their antecedents and related primates, and their cultural behavior and institutions in comparative perspective. Includes instruction in biological/physical anthropology; primatology; human paleontology and prehistoric archeology; hominid evolution; anthropological linguistics; ethnography; ethnology; ethnohistory; sociocultural anthropology; psychological anthropology; research methods; and applications to areas such as medicine, forensic pathology, museum studies, and international affairs.

Archeology: A program that focuses on the systematic study of extinct societies, and the past of living societies, via the excavation, analysis, and interpretation of their artifactual, human, and associated remains. Includes instruction in archeological theory, field methods, dating methods, conservation and museum studies, cultural and physical evolution, and the study of specific selected past cultures.

Astronomy: A general program that focuses on the planetary, galactic, and stellar phenomena occurring in outer space. Includes instruction in celestial mechanics; cosmology; stellar physics; galactic evolution; quasars; stellar distribution and motion; interstellar medium; atomic and molecular constituents of astronomical phenomena; planetary science; solar system evolution; and specific methodologies such as optical astronomy, radioastronomy, and theoretical astronomy.

Astrophysics: A program that focuses on the theoretical and observational study of the structure, properties, and behavior of stars, star systems and clusters, stellar life cycles, and related phenomena. Includes instruction in cosmology, plasma kinetics, stellar physics, convolution and nonequilibrium radiation transfer theory, non-Euclidean geometries, mathematical modeling, galactic structure theory, and relativistic astronomy.

Atmospheric Chemistry and Climatology: A program that focuses on the scientific study of atmospheric constituents, reactions, measurement techniques, and processes in predictive, current, and historical contexts. Includes instruction in climate modeling, gases and aerosols, trace gases, aqueous phase chemistry, sinks, transport mechanisms, computer measurement, climate variability, paleoclimatology, climate diagnosis, numerical modeling and data analysis, ionization, recombination, photoemission, and plasma chemistry.

Atmospheric Physics and Dynamics: A program that focuses on the scientific study of the processes governing the interactions, movement, and behavior of atmospheric phenomena and related terrestrial and solar phenomena. Includes instruction in cloud and precipitation physics, solar radiation transfer, active and passive remote sensing, atmospheric electricity and acoustics, atmospheric wave phenomena, turbulence and boundary layers, solar wind, geomagnetic storms, coupling, natural plasma, and energization.

Atmospheric Sciences and Meteorology: A general program that focuses on the scientific study of the composition and behavior of the atmospheric envelopes surrounding the earth, the effect of earth's atmosphere on terrestrial weather, and related problems of environment and climate. Includes instruction in atmospheric chemistry and physics; atmospheric dynamics; climatology and climate change; weather simulation; weather forecasting; climate modeling and mathematical theory; and studies of specific phenomena such as clouds, weather systems, storms, and precipitation patterns.

Biochemistry/Biophysics and Molecular Biology: An integrated, combined program that focuses on the structure, function, and dynamic behavior of the components of biological systems at the submolecular, molecular, and supramolecular levels and their influence on biological activity at the cellular, tissue, organ, and organismic levels. Includes instruction in biochemistry, biophysics, structural biology, molecular biology, and research applications and methods appropriate to specific topics.

Botany/Plant Biology: A program that focuses on the scientific study of plants, related microbial organisms, and plant habitats and ecosystem relations. Includes instruction in plant anatomy and structure, phytochemistry, cytology, plant genetics, plant morphology and physiology, plant ecology, plant taxonomy and systematics, paleobotany, and applications of biophysics and molecular biology.

Cartography: A program that focuses on the systematic study of mapmaking and the application of mathematical, computer, and other techniques to the science of mapping geographic information. Includes instruction in cartographic theory and map projections; computer-assisted cartography; map design and layout; photogrammetry; air photo interpretation; remote sensing; cartographic editing; and applications to specific industrial, commercial, research, and governmental mapping problems.

Chemical Physics: A program that focuses on the scientific study of structural phenomena combining the disciplines of physical chemistry and atomic/molecular physics. Includes instruction in heterogeneous structures, alignment and surface phenomena, quantum theory, mathematical physics, statistical and classical mechanics, chemical kinetics, liquid crystals and membranes, molecular synthesis and design, and laser physics.

Chemistry: A general program that focuses on the scientific study of the composition and behavior of matter, including its micro- and macrostructure, the processes of chemical change, and the theoretical description and laboratory simulation of these phenomena.

Ecology: A program that focuses on the scientific study of the relationships and interactions of small-scale biological systems, such as organisms, to each other, to complex and whole systems, and to the physical and other nonbiological aspects of their environments. Includes instruction in biogeochemistry; landscape and/or marine/aquatic dynamics; decomposition; global and regional elemental budgets; biotic and abiotic regulation of nutrient cycles; ecophysiology; ecosystem resilience, disturbance, and succession; community and habitat dynamics; organismal interactions (co-evolution, competition, predation); paleoecology; and evolutionary ecology.

Economics: A general program that focuses on the systematic study of the production, conservation, and allocation of resources in conditions of scarcity, together with the organizational frameworks related to these processes. Includes instruction in economic theory, micro- and macroeconomics, comparative economic systems, money and banking systems, international economics, quantitative analytical methods, and applications to specific industries and public policy issues.

Engineering: A program that generally prepares individuals to apply mathematical and scientific principles to solve a wide variety of practical problems in industry, social organization, public works, and commerce.

Engineering Science: A program with a general focus on the general application of various combinations of mathematical and scientific principles to the analysis and evaluation of engineering problems, including applied research in human behavior, statistics, biology, chemistry, the earth and planetary sciences, atmospherics and meteorology, and computer applications.

Entomology: A program that focuses on the scientific study of insect species and populations in respect of their life cycles, morphology, genetics, physiology, ecology, taxonomy, population dynamics, and environmental and economic impacts. Includes instruction in biological and physical sciences as well as insect toxicology and the biochemical control of insect populations.

Exercise Physiology: A program that focuses on the scientific study of the physiological processes involved in physical or motor activity, including sensorimotor interactions; response mechanisms; and the effects of injury, disease, and disability. Includes instruction in muscular and skeletal anatomy; molecular and cellular basis of muscle contraction; fuel utilization; neurophysiology of motor mechanics; systemic physiological responses (respiration, blood flow, endocrine secretions, and others); fatigue and exhaustion; muscle and body training; physiology of specific exercises and activities; physiology of injury; and the effects of disabilities and disease.

Genetics: A general program that focuses on the scientific study of the organization, recombination, function, regulation, and transmission of heritable information in biological organisms at all levels of complexity. Includes instruction in Mendelian genetics, mechanisms of gene regulation, chromosome structure and replication, epigenetic phenomena, DNA repair and recombination, sex determination, genetic interactions between genomes, and molecular evolution.

Geochemistry and Petrology: A program that focuses on the scientific study of the igneous, metamorphic, and hydrothermal processes within the earth and the mineral, fluid, rock, and ore deposits resulting from them. Includes instruction in mineralogy, crystallography, petrology, volcanology, economic geology, meteoritics, geochemical reactions, deposition, compound transformation, core studies, theoretical geochemistry, computer applications, and laboratory studies.

Geography: A program that focuses on the systematic study of the spatial distribution and interrelationships of people, natural resources, and plant and animal life. Includes instruction in historical and political geography; cultural geography; economic and physical geography; regional science; cartographic methods; remote sensing; spatial analysis; and applications to areas such as land-use planning, development studies, and analyses of specific countries, regions, and resources.

Geology/Earth Science: A program that focuses on the scientific study of the earth; the forces acting upon it; and the behavior of the solids, liquids, and gases comprising it. Includes instruction in historical geology, geomorphology, and sedimentology; the chemistry of rocks and soils; stratigraphy; mineralogy; petrology; geostatistics; volcanology; glaciology; geophysical principles; and applications to research and industrial problems.

Geophysics and Seismology: A program that focuses on the scientific study of the physics of solids and its application to the study of the earth and other planets. Includes instruction in gravimetric, seismology, earthquake forecasting, magnetometry, electrical properties of solid bodies, plate tectonics, active deformation, thermodynamics, remote sensing, geodesy, and laboratory simulations of geological processes.

Hydrology and Water Resources Science: A program that focuses on the scientific of study of the occurrence, circulation, distribution, chemical and physical properties, and environmental interaction of surface and subsurface waters, including groundwater. Includes instruction in geophysics, thermodynamics, fluid mechanics, chemical physics, geomorphology, mathematical modeling, hydrologic analysis, continental water processes, global water balance, and environmental science.

Marine Biology and Biological Oceanography: A program that focuses on the scientific study of the ecology and behavior of microbes, plants, and animals inhabiting oceans, coastal waters, and saltwater wetlands and their interactions with the physical environment. Includes instruction in chemical, physical, and geological oceanography; molecular, cellular, and biochemical studies; marine microbiology; marine botany; ichthyology; mammalogy; marine population dynamics and biodiversity; reproductive biology; studies of specific species, phyla, habitats, and ecosystems; marine paleoecology and paleontology; and applications to fields such as fisheries science and biotechnology.

Materials Science: A program that focuses on the general application of mathematical and scientific principles to the analysis and evaluation of the characteristics and behavior of solids, including internal structure, chemical properties, transport and energy flow properties, thermodynamics of solids, stress and failure factors, chemical transformation states and processes, compound materials, and research on industrial applications of specific materials.

Mathematics: A general program that focuses on the analysis of quantities, magnitudes, forms, and their relationships, using symbolic logic and language. Includes instruction in algebra, calculus, functional analysis, geometry, number theory, logic, topology, and other mathematical specializations.

Meteorology: A program that focuses on the scientific study of the prediction of atmospheric motion and climate change. Includes instruction in general circulation patterns, weather phenomena, atmospheric predictability, parameterization, numerical and statistical analysis, large- and mesoscale phenomena, kinematic structures, precipitation processes, and forecasting techniques.

Microbiology: A program that focuses on the scientific study of unicellular organisms and colonies, and subcellular genetic matter and their ecological interactions with human beings and other life. Includes instruction in microbial genetics, cell biology, cell physiology, virology, pathogenic microbiology, environmental microbiology, immunology, biostatistics, bioinformatics, and laboratory methods including microscopy.

Oceanography, Chemical and Physical: A program that focuses on the scientific study of the chemical components, mechanisms, structure, and movement of ocean waters and their interaction with terrestrial and atmospheric phenomena. Includes instruction in material inputs and outputs, chemical and biochemical transformations in marine systems, equilibria studies, inorganic and organic ocean chemistry, oceanographic processes, sediment transport, zone processes, circulation, mixing, tidal movements, wave properties, and seawater properties.

Optics/Optical Sciences: A program that focuses on the scientific study of light energy, including its structure, properties, and behavior under different conditions. Includes instruction in wave theory, wave mechanics, electromagnetic theory, physical optics, geometric optics, quantum theory of light, photon detecting, laser theory, wall and beam properties, chaotic light, nonlinear optics, harmonic generation, optical systems theory, and applications to engineering problems.

Paleontology: A program that focuses on the scientific study of extinct life forms and associated fossil remains, and the reconstruction and analysis of ancient life forms, ecosystems, and geologic processes. Includes instruction in sedimentation and fossilization processes, fossil chemistry, evolutionary biology, paleoecology, paleoclimatology, trace fossils, micropaleontology, invertebrate paleontology, vertebrate paleontology, paleobotany, field research methods, and laboratory research and conservation methods.

Physical Sciences: A program that focuses on the major topics, concepts, processes, and interrelationships of physical phenomena as studied in any combination of physical science disciplines.

Physics: A general program that focuses on the scientific study of matter and energy and the formulation and testing of the laws governing the behavior of the matter-energy continuum. Includes instruction in classical and modern physics, electricity and magnetism, thermodynamics, mechanics, wave properties, nuclear processes, relativity and quantum theory, quantitative methods, and laboratory methods.

Planetary Astronomy and Science: A program that focuses on the scientific study of planets, small objects, and related gravitational systems. Includes instruction in the structure and composition of planetary surfaces and interiors, planetary atmospheres, satellites, orbital mechanics, asteroids and comets, solar system evolution and dynamics, planetary evolution, gravitational physics, and radiation physics.

Statistics: A general program that focuses on the relationships between groups of measurements, and similarities and differences, using probability theory and techniques derived from it. Includes instruction in the principles in probability theory, binomial distribution, regression analysis, standard deviation, stochastic processes, Monte Carlo method, Bayesian statistics, nonparametric statistics, sampling theory, and statistical techniques.

Wildlife Biology: A program that focuses on the application of biological principles to the study of vertebrate wildlife, wildlife habitats, and related ecosystems in remote and urban areas. Includes instruction in animal ecology; adaptational biology; urban ecosystems; natural and artificial habitat management; limnology; wildlife pathology; and vertebrate zoological specializations such as mammalogy, herpetology, ichthyology, ornithology, and others.

Zoology/Animal Biology: A general program that focuses on the scientific study of the biology of animal species and phyla, with reference to their molecular and cellular systems, anatomy, physiology, and behavior. Includes instruction in molecular and cell biology, microbiology, anatomy and physiology, ecology and behavior, evolutionary biology, and applications to specific species and phyla.

Transportation, Distribution, and Logistics

This career cluster includes majors that appeal to students with an interest in operations that move people or materials.

Aeronautics/Aviation/Aerospace Science and Technology: A program that focuses on the general study of aviation and the aviation industry, including in-flight and ground support operations. Includes instruction in the technical, business, and general aspects of air transportation systems.

Agricultural Mechanics and Equipment/Machine Technology: A program that prepares individuals to maintain and repair specialized farm, ranch, and agribusiness power equipment and vehicles. Includes instruction in the principles of diesel, combustion, electrical, steam, hydraulic, and mechanical systems and their application to the maintenance of terrestrial and airborne crop spraying equipment; tractors and hauling equipment; planting and harvesting equipment; cutting equipment; power sources and systems for silos; irrigation and pumping equipment; dairy, feeding, and shearing operations; and processing systems.

Air Traffic Controller: A program that prepares individuals to apply technical knowledge and skills to air traffic management and control, usually with additional training at the FAA Flight Control Center in a cooperative education program. Includes instruction in flight control, the use of radar and electronic scanning devices, plotting of flights, radio communication, interpretation of weather conditions affecting flights, flight instrumentation used by pilots, and maintenance of flight-control center or control-tower log books.

Aircraft Power Plant Technology: A program that prepares individuals to apply technical knowledge and skills to repair, service, and maintain all types of aircraft power plant and related systems. Instruction includes engine inspection and maintenance, lubrication and cooling, electrical and ignition systems, carburetion, fuels and fuel systems, and propeller and fan assemblies.

Airframe Mechanics and Aircraft Maintenance Technology: A program that prepares individuals to apply technical knowledge and skills to repair, service, and maintain all aircraft components other than engines, propellers, avionics, and instruments. Includes instruction in layout and fabrication of sheet metal, fabric, wood, and other materials into structural members, parts, and fittings and replacement of damaged or worn parts such as control cables and hydraulic units.

Airline/Commercial/Professional Pilot and Flight Crew: A program that prepares individuals to apply technical knowledge and skills to the flying and/or navigation of commercial passenger and cargo, agricultural, public service, corporate, and rescue fixed-wing aircraft. Includes instruction in principles of aircraft design and performance, aircraft flight systems and controls, flight crew operations and procedures, radio communications, navigation procedures and systems, airways safety and traffic regulations, and governmental rules and regulations pertaining to piloting aircraft. Programs may qualify individuals to sit for the FAA commercial and airline aircrew examinations.

Alternative Fuel Vehicle Technology: A program that prepares individuals to apply technical knowledge and skills to the maintenance of alternative fuel vehicles and the conversion of standard vehicles to AFV status. Includes instruction in electrical vehicles, liquefied petroleum gas (LPG) vehicles, compressed natural gas (CNG) vehicles, hybrid fuel technology, electrical and electronic systems, engine performance, diagnosis and repair, and conversion/installation.

Automobile/Automotive Mechanics Technology: A program that prepares individuals to apply technical knowledge and skills to repair, service, and maintain all types of automobiles. Includes instruction in brake systems, electrical systems, engine performance, engine repair, suspension and steering, automatic and manual transmissions and drive trains, and heating and air condition systems.

Aviation/Airway Management and Operations: A program that prepares individuals to apply technical knowledge and skills to the management of aviation industry operations and services. Includes instruction in airport operations, ground traffic direction, ground support and flightline operations, passenger and cargo operations, flight safety and security operations, aviation industry regulation, and related business aspects of managing aviation enterprises.

Avionics Maintenance Technology: A program that prepares individuals to apply technical knowledge and skills to repair, service, and maintain all types of aircraft operating, control, and electronic systems. Includes instruction in flight instrumentation, aircraft communications and homing systems, radar and other sensory systems, navigation aids, and specialized systems for various types of civilian and military aircraft.

Bicycle Mechanics and Repair Technology: A program that prepares individuals to apply technical knowledge and skills to repair, service, and maintain bicycles and other human-powered vehicles. Includes instruction in lubrication, adjustments of moving parts, and wheel building.

Diesel Mechanics Technology: A program that prepares individuals to apply technical knowledge and skills to repair, service, and maintain diesel engines in vehicles such as automobiles, buses, ships, trucks, railroad locomotives, and construction equipment; as well as stationary diesel engines in electrical generators and related equipment.

Diver, Professional and Instructor: A program that prepares individuals to apply technical knowledge and skills to function as professional deep-water or scuba divers, diving instructors, or diving support personnel. Includes instruction in the use of diving equipment and related specialized gear; diving safety procedures; operation and maintenance of underwater life-support systems; underwater communication systems; decompression systems; underwater salvage; exploration, rescue, and photography; and installation and fitting of underwater mechanical systems and their maintenance, repair, or demolition.

Driver and Safety Teacher Education: A program that prepares individuals to teach driver and safety education programs at various educational levels.

Engine Machinist: A program that prepares individuals to apply technical knowledge and skills to the building and reconstruction of automotive and commercial vehicle engines. Includes instruction in cylinder head and block, crack repair, crankshaft inspection and repair, connecting rods and pistons, balancing, block preparation, disassembly and repair, engine assembly, gas and diesel technology, and inspection and machining.

Flight Instructor: A program that prepares individuals to apply technical knowledge and skills to the training pilot or navigators to fly and/or navigate commercial passenger and cargo, agricultural, public service, corporate and rescue aircraft, fixed or rotary wing. Includes instruction in principles of aircraft design and performance, aircraft flight systems and controls, flight crew operations and procedures, radio communications and navigation procedures and systems, airways safety and traffic regulations, and governmental rules and regulations pertaining to piloting aircraft. Programs may qualify individuals to administer the FAA commercial air crew examinations.

Heavy Equipment Maintenance Technology: A program that prepares individuals to apply technical knowledge and skills in the field maintenance and repair of heavy equipment, and in the general maintenance and overhaul of such equipment. Includes instruction in inspection, maintenance, and repair of tracks, wheels, brakes, operating controls, pneumatic and hydraulic systems, electrical circuitry, and engines and in techniques of welding and brazing.

Industrial Mechanics and Maintenance Technology: A program that prepares individuals to apply technical knowledge and skills to repair and maintain industrial machinery and equipment such as cranes, pumps, engines and motors, pneumatic tools, conveyor systems, production machinery, marine deck machinery, and steam propulsion, refinery, and pipeline-distribution systems.

Marine Maintenance/Fitter and Ship Repair Technology: A program that prepares individuals to apply technical knowledge and skills to repair outboard and inboard engines; test, maintain, and repair steering devices and electrical systems; repair metal, wood, and fiberglass hulls and vessel components; fabricate and maintain sails; and repair and balance propellers and drive shafts.

Marine Science/Merchant Marine Officer: A program that prepares individuals to serve as captains, executive officers, engineers, and ranking mates on commercially licensed inland, coastal, and ocean-going vessels. Includes instruction in maritime traditions and law, maritime policy, economics and management of commercial marine operations, basic naval architecture and engineering, shipboard power systems engineering, crew supervision, and administrative procedures.

Medium/Heavy Vehicle and Truck Technology: A program that prepares individuals to apply technical knowledge and skills to the specialized maintenance and repair of trucks, buses, and other commercial and industrial vehicles. Includes instruction in diesel engine mechanics, suspension and steering, brake systems, electrical and electronic systems, preventive maintenance inspections, drive trains, gasoline engine mechanics, HVAC systems, and auxiliary equipment installation and repair.

Motorcycle Maintenance and Repair Technology: A program that prepares individuals to apply technical knowledge and skills to repair, service, and maintain motorcycles and other similar powered vehicles. Includes instruction in lubrication and cooling systems, electrical and ignition systems, carburetion, fuel systems, and adjustments of moving parts.

Small-Engine Mechanics and Repair Technology: A program that prepares individuals to apply technical knowledge and skills to repair, service, and maintain small internal-combustion engines used on portable power equipment such as lawnmowers, chain saws, rotary tillers, and snow-mobiles.

Transportation Management: A program that prepares individuals to plan, administer, and coordinate physical transportation operations, networks, and systems. Includes instruction in transportation systems and technologies; traffic logistics and engineering; multi- and intermodal transportation systems; regional integration; facilities design and construction; transportation planning and finance; demand analysis and forecasting; carrier management; behavioral issues; transportation policy and law; intelligent systems; and applications to aviation, maritime, rail, and highway facilities and systems.

Vehicle Emissions Inspection and Maintenance Technology: A program that prepares individuals to apply technical knowledge and skills to test, repair, service, and maintain vehicle emission systems in accordance with relevant laws and regulations.

Index